PAUL HALLAM

I0094741

has written or co-written several screenplays including *A Kind of English* (Ruhul Amin), *Caught Looking* (Constantine Giannaris), *Nighthawks, Strip Jack Naked* (Ron Peck) and Cannes Critics' Prize winner *Young Soul Rebels* (Isaac Julien). The script of the film was published by the British Film Institute in *Diary of a Young Soul Rebel*. His play, *The Dish*, was performed in London, New York and Toronto. A BBC Radio 4 adaptation of *The Dish* was broadcast in 1998. In the late 1970s he was part of the independent film group, Four Corners. The group set up a cinema and film workshop in Bethnal Green, London. ¶Many of his essays, articles and reviews have appeared in a range of books, journals and magazines. His first book, *The Book of Sodom* (Verso) is a very personal look at the idea of the "wicked city". The book emerged from a repeated city walk in Clerkenwell, London. He wrote the title essay for *Estate*, a Fugitive Images book. ¶In recent years Paul has collaborated on many short films, *Soho*, a film by Ron Peck and Paul Hallam, *King's Cross*, a film by Kate Boyd and Paul Hallam, and the autobiographical *The Last Biscuit* (Paul Hallam and Andrea Luka Zimmerman). ¶He was a Writer in Residence, and cultural studies tutor at Central Saint Martins College of Art and Design. He moved to Istanbul in 2008, and taught at Istanbul University. He recently left teaching to focus on new writing. ¶He is at work on a new book, and a feature film set in Turkey, provisionally titled *The Turkish Dormitory* and a second project around Charles Laughton. He has also been a script advisor on a new feature length documentary about Yılmaz Güney by İlker Savaşkurt, *Ballad of the Exiles*. All of these recent projects are in collaboration with the producer, Abbas Nokhasteh (Openvizor). ¶The extensive Paul Hallam Archive (also in collaboration with Openvizor) is housed at the Bishopsgate Institute in London. A series of films concerning the Archive and archiving have recently been produced. ¶In 2015 Paul entered into collaboration with Metaflux Publishing to republish, redesign and newly introduce some of his earlier work, but also to produce new work around sexuality.

PAUL HALLAM

IF YOU LOOK AT IT LONG ENOUGH...

Metaflux 2015

METAFLUX // INCANDESCENT BODIES

If you look at it long enough...
©2004 Paul Hallam
First published in the
Journal of Homosexuality, 47:3-4, pp59-74

1. Gay Culture; 2. Pornography; 3. Philosophy

Keystrokes
©2015 Gary Wickham
gwickham@rcn.com

Monography
©2015 Paul Hallam
paulehallam@gmail.com

This edition ©2015 Metaflux Publishing
Edited by Rodrigo Maltez Novaes
Art and Design by Chagrin
Published by Metaflux Publishing
www.metafluxpublishing.com

ISBN 978 0 9933272 2 3

```
ZZOZZOOOO88888DD88OOOOZZ$777777$$=................................:~+??=:::::::::::::::~~~=≡++??7
888888DDDDDDDNNNDDDD88OOOZ$$$7I77$I....................,::,,,,:,=??+~:::::::::::::::::::~~~=
DDDDDDDNNNNNNNNNNNNNNNDDDD88OZ$$77I77$?.............,,,::::~~:::,,,,,,,=??+=~~~=I+=::::::::::~~~~~=?
DNNNNNNNNNNNNNNNNNNNNNNDDDD88OZ$$77$$Z+.............,::::::::,,,,,,,=7$I+=~+I+=:::::::::::~~~~~~~≡
NNNNNNNNNNNNNMMMNNNNNNNNNNDDDD8OZ$$$$$7,..........,::::,,,,,,:~~=+I?++=+?I+=::::::~~~~~~~~=
NNNNNNO?IDNMMMMMMMMMMMMMMNNNNDD8OOZZ$ZZ,.........,:::,,,,,::::~=≡≡~~=≡≡I$+=~~~~~~~~≡≡≡≡+7
NN?.......:~=NMMMMMMM~,?DNNNNNNNNDDD88OZZZ,.........,::::,,,::~~:::::~~=≡I$?=~~~~~~~~~~≡≡≡+
............~MMMMMMMN=.,MMMMNNNNNDDD8OOZO7............,:::::,,,::::::::≡=+IZ?=::~~~~~~≡≡≡+
............,~MMMMMMMZ,MMMMMNNNNNNDDD88OO$=...........,:::::::,,,,::::::::≡=+IZI=~~~~~≡≡+?I
.......,,,:~7MMMMMMM?MMMMMMNNNNNNNDDD8OOZ$,.........,:::::::::,~::,,::::::~?+=7O7+~~=≡≡
......:~:....~NMMMMMMN8MMMMMMNNNNNNNNDDD888+.........,::::::~~::::,,:::::~?+~7O$?~=≡≡≡++
.......=$7=:...~$8D8+.IMMMMMNNDZ:8DNDDDDD8O,.........,::,,,,::~~~:::::,,:~?+~~78Z7=
888OZO88Z77I?Z....~+~,,,,NMMMMMNDZ,,,,=++++=~,,......,::~~:::::,:,,,,,:::~?~7DO$=
$$7$OZ$$77I??+O...=~,,,.8MMMMNN7,......~=.....,,,....,:~~:::::,,,,,,,,,,,~?I~7DOZ=
Z$7??7$$$777$ZZZ8??+++=::,,,:DNNN8=,,,,,::,,,=++::,,,.....,:~~~::::,,,,,,,:,,:::~??7
$$$7$$7$OOZ≡≡≡≡≡≡≡≡≡≡≡≡≡≡≡≡≡≡≡≡≡≡≡≡≡≡≡≡≡≡≡≡≡≡≡≡≡≡≡≡≡≡≡≡≡≡≡≡≡≡≡≡≡≡≡≡≡≡≡≡≡≡:::~I$I
OZOO88ZZ888888 88II7OO$ZII???7I$Z$=?+= ,,,,:~:,~+7=~~,,,,,:::~~~≡≡≡≡≡:::::::::≡~IZ$+
OO888D88DDD8888 8Z?==~~O88N88ZI+~~:,,?I+~~=~:,,,......+=,,,,,,,,:~=:~~:~~::::::::≡:≡
88DDDDDDDDD888 I+++=~$ND8IIIII?=:,,=?+~..,,,,,,,,,:~=~?=,,,~=:,,,:~~=I::::,:::::
DDDDDDDDDNNNDO ZOO8DD8ZNND888DDD8$=:,≡=I:,,,,:~~=:,,=++=~,,:~~=~:,,~:~~~~~
NDNDNNNDDDNND7$77I?++==+NNNZZ$7+=~:,,,I?II+=~:,,~~?,,,,,,~~:,,~=~~:,,~=≡≡≡≡≡≡+~:,~=
NNNNNNNDD$7NNDOI???++++I$8NN7+?II7++788Z?$O==~:::,,,,~~=+?,,,:~~:~~~,,,,,,:~~≡≡≡≡≡+≡:,~=
NNNND$I77$8MNNDDD8888$IIINDDD8888DDZI?+=$OO:,,,,~,,,,++=~,,,,,,,,,,:~~~~~::~:~~≡≡≡≡+I++~~~~
NOI??I77$$ZNNN$$ZOO$777I?ZDD8=?≡≡≡≡=~~:,:8Z+~,,,,,,,,+=~?,,,,:~~:~:~~~~~~≡~:~~~~≡≡+
8OZZOZO8888MNN7+++≡≡≡~~N8O=::::,,,,,,Z$=+,,,,,,,,,:=~+?=:,,:::~=:,,~~~~:,,,,,,,,,,
ND8DDDDD88DNMNNZ???++?+~:,=8O$~::~~~~~:,,=+?:,,,:~::,,,=+?=~:,::::≡=~::+=~,,:~::,,,:::
MMNN8Z7?+==≡≡MMD?,,,,,,,,,,~$=?,,,,,,,,:++~,,,,~:,,:≡=~=,,,,,,,:~:,,~~~:,,:~=≡≡+++
8ZI+~::::,:DM8$::::~~~~~:$+?+:,,,?II?=~,,,,:~~?+~:,,,,,,,:~~?+~,,:::~~~~:≡≡≡≡~~~~~
?=≡~:,,,,,:IMOI=::,,,,,,,:,I7+~=:,,,~=≡≡~:,,~=≡~:,~~::~~~~~~:,,,,::~:,≡≡≡≡≡≡≡≡~
≡=~~:,,,,,,=MO7~,........,??=~,,,,,,,,~+≡+=~:,,:~~~::≡=~+?,,,~~~::,,,~~=≡≡≡++≡≡
=~~::::::::~8OI?,,,,,,,,,:,~?=+:~,,,,,~+≡=~::,,:~=~:,::≡=~:,,,,,::~~~~:,,~=≡≡+++≡=~~~
=~~:::::::::IN$7+====~~~~:::+?++::,,:~~=≡≡=~:,::~=~:,:,,:~~?++~,,,,,,:≡~:,:~=≡+?????
≡=~~:::::::::+NZI+::,,,,,,:,,:+++≡~=:,,~:=≡≡~::::~=~:,,~:,,,,:~~?+=~,,,,,,~=+?????+?
≡=~~::::::::::=88I+,,,,,,,,,,,,~+I=:,,,:~=~::::,,:~=~:,,:::~~~?++=~:,,,,,,,:≡=≡≡≡≡≡~
~=~~~~~~~~~~~=OD7I~,,,,,,,,,,,,,~+?~::::~~~~::::::~=~:,:::::,~=?+=~,,,,,,,,,,:~=+?7++?
≡=+++++≡≡≡~~~7NO7+====≡≡≡≡≡≡≡≡≡=?II?=:,,,,:~~~~~~=≡~:,,,,,,,,,:~=?I?=~,,,,,,,,,,:,::~=+
??++≡~:::::::::+88$?+~~~~~~:~:::~~:~?II?=~~~~:::,:,,~?+~:,,,,,~=?I?=:,,,,,,:,,,,,:,::+???
+≡≡~~~::::::::=$D$?=~::::::::+I??+~:,,,,,,,,,=?I≡=~~~::::,,,~:≡+II?=~~~:,,,,,,,,,,,~=≡
≡=~~::::::::::~I8ZI+::,,,,,,,,~?7I+~:,,,,,,~+I?+~::,,,,~:::~+?+≡~:~~:,,,,,,,,,,,,,~=≡+
≡=~~::::::::::~IDDZI=~:::::::~~≡≡I77I+~,,,,~+I?+~:,,,,,,,::~=≡=II?+~:~~:,,,,,,,,,,,,,,,,:
≡≡≡≡~~~:::::::~?8NO$?≡≡≡≡≡≡≡≡≡≡≡+7Z$I+~:::::~~~=~~=~+?I?=:,,,,,,,,,,,,,:~=≡+?7$$I+~:::,,,,,,,,,,,,:
```

KEYSTROKES

¶Love is sometimes conceived as the opposite of desire. This is not just because familiarity and repetition can dull the sharp point of desire, wear it down, erode its ability to prick and sting us to life. Part of what I mean when I tell you I love you is that I'm filled to bursting with you, that you are everything to me, that you complete me. In wanting you, however, I'm confronted by the knotty nature of the wholeness romantic love both requires and promises to enact. The logic of desire is one of displacement and deferral, of longing and lack. Closer to the mark, perhaps, desire is nothing but this very lack. Evasive and waggish, Eros seems able to thwart every attempt to wiggle free of him, sticking around to confound and confuse my best efforts to join with you in love. ¶But what happens if we renounce the idea of love as fusion or communion, as desire's remedy? What if we brace ourselves firmly in the space opened up by desire, refusing to flinch away toward the comfort of a cure? This thought emerges as a kind of thematic roadhouse, a narrative nub, in many of Paul Hallam's writings, plays and films. And it's against this backdrop that the book you've just cracked open figures as one of its most deliberate and distilled elaborations, a deliciously personal and tawdry twirl through one writer's pleasure palace of porn. ¶In the Internet age, of course, it isn't possible (if it ever was) to think about or to consume pornography as a fully defined and self-contained set of practices relegated to the horizon of everyday life. No longer in need of liberation from a shoebox in the back of the cupboard, porn has marched decisively out of the closets and into the streets. In fact, in a relatively recent and dizzying inversion of more priggish times, plugged-in people have to make a special (though ultimately fruitless) effort not to see porn. What does it say about us, then, that we expect a certain amount of shame, contrition or denial from folks (ourselves included) who get caught in the act of watching? What, in other words, continues to be embarrassing about porn? ¶Surely, there are a number of tricks we can turn here (rhetorically, anyhow) to help flesh out a preliminary response. For one thing, free market economies have a tendency to represent watching – like reading, listening or thinking – as a passive and scandalously nonproductive engagement with the world. In this context, consuming porn gets coded as a refusal to discipline your desire in the service of socially or economically productive ends. Viewing porn (or books about it, try reading this one to your boss) doesn't constitute proper work – the only thing, to this way of thinking, with an intrinsic social value. Like studying philosophy or going to the ballet, porn is strictly for wastrels and wankers. ¶For erotic disciplinarians, however, the pornification of culture represents an even more alarming, if amorphous, threat: The inexhaustibility of desire. People from Western societies, with roots in Christian ideals of redemption

and unconditional love, tend to experience desire as a hole that needs plug-
ging. In the absence of a firm hand,
Eros invariably opens himself up wide,
exposing the gaping gash, the existential
nothingness, which separates the moral
from the made-up. Desire that is not
clearly managed and channeled (into
marriage, say, or religion or work) sig-
nifies a deeply unsettling and shameful
refusal to be domesticated or redeemed,
a renunciation of the saucy seductions
of both capitalism and Christianity. ¶It's
a bit baffling, in this context, to witness
the recent, balls-out efforts by defenders
of discipline to try to exclude Ls and
Gs (and some Bs and Ts) from marriage.
Marrying us off, after all, would seem
to be the ideal social prophylactic for
containing and dispensing with rogue
desires. It turns out, though, that the
impulse to democratize the institution
of marriage only ends up highlighting
the inexhaustible iterability of love and
desire. If two queers can marry each
other, then why not three or four? In the
end, what's to stop you from marrying

Gary Wickham

Keystrokes

your goldfish, or your granny? What, indeed. The slipperiness of this slope tends to get construed, quite rightly, as the desperate ranting of cultural luddites, hands on hips, refusing to get with the times. But perhaps there's more to it than that. Making the case for keeping people (and desires) out not only tends to sound wayward and wacky. It works against its own explicit intentions by unsettling the idea that there is some sort of originary truth of desire prior to its enunciation. It suggests, despite itself, that romantic love is not so much desire's telos or target, as one of its contingent, inexhaustibly many, trajectories. ¶This shift in perspective is significant, subversive even, because, as Hallam's fantasies and reflections reveal, it helps us join up the contingency and multiplicity of erotic desire with the desire to understand, to reckon with, to come to terms. Of all the scenes contained in this shrewd and sexy little book, I think the one that titillates me the most is our slightly wicked author's depiction of his porn fantasy home (tip: resist the urge to flip ahead): A place where memory, wisdom and desire have the bloody hots for one another; where shagging, recollecting and knowing are one big tangled, sweaty mess. Who knows, then? Maybe there's some room for philosophers, after all. I just know I want to go there. Right now.

Gary Wickham
July 2015
Brooklyn, New York

¶Gary Wickham graduated with honors in philosophy from Miami University of Ohio in 1990. He subsequently received a Ph.D in philosophy from the State University of New York at Binghamton in 1997, and an M.S.W. from Hunter College in 1998. A Licensed Clinical Social Worker (LCSW-R), Gary has been living and working in New York City since then, most recently as the Director of an Office of Mental Health-licensed supportive housing program in Midtown Manhattan. He also donates time reviewing and cataloging archival material at the LGBT Community Center National History Archive.

Paul Hallam

IF YOU LOOK AT IT
LONG ENOUGH...

¶And how might I discuss my near daily dose of pornography, since pornography links my past to the present, the present of the watching of the porn, and links that present to future desires? Links pleasure to regret, memory to fantasy. It is also intensely personal, almost comically so. I found myself, on the rough draft, censoring myself. As if I didn't want anyone to know; porn as the last vestige of privacy. I've enjoyed porn since I was ten, few days have passed without a glance, or a more sustained, and often stained look at it. Why then do I find it so difficult to give it proper consideration? Why do I slightly hesitate over the word "enjoyed"? ¶I wonder about the reader, the one who buys or borrows this publication. And I'm curious about the contributors. Who might use the frowned upon "I" in their essay; declare an interest? Who will remain detached? Who will celebrate "self-abuse," my favourite term for wanking? I will be looking through this seminal issue in search of the "I" (the abused selves amongst you making notes)."Wank," that most common of the British terms for the act that usually, but not always, accompanies the viewing, is useful and direct and yet it displeases me. Sometimes we watch, buttoned up, with friends. Sometimes we laugh, sometimes porn is just a kind of back-drop, a pleasingly repetitive wallpaper. I find watching porn enjoyable whilst ironing for example, but I wouldn't risk a combination of the two activities. "Jerk-off" too displeases me, it sounds too hurried and erratic, and the one hundred other terms. Slang dictionaries have pages of them. Mostly embarrassed words, comic-edged. I will stick to the condemnatory and curious "self-abuse." If the academic abused selves don't appear in this journal, this record, I will be disappointed. I hope that some of you, at least, will admit to porn's fasci-nation and submit to its seduction. ¶Do words in an academic journal or in a book categorised "Gay Studies" have the same seductive power for you as, say, the videos you might hold in your collection? I trust that you have read or watched gay porn, that you have enjoyed it, and I wonder about your experience of it. I can only tell you about my own search for porn, from soft to hard, from porn disguised in academic tomes to the dirty bits of great literature. Even in charts, statistics and sociological surveys. A relentless search over decades, though I've cut down now; there is so much of it, too much of it on the internet (too much for me I mean, I'm glad it's there). Not unlike, I suspect, many a newcomer to the internet, a few years ago my days were devoted to joining "Groups." I received hundreds of photos, some sought out or requested, others just turned up as if by magic. I was caught up in the semi-fictional games of the chat rooms and found myself awake far too often at 4am. The addiction soon wore off. ¶Though porn is clearly marketed, targeted to appeal to a wide or a more selective but still substantial market, what I see in my videos, and look at in my porn collection, is not, of course, what you would see. I collect dirty videos. I have magazines and porn stories, photo porn kept for thirty years now, sometimes older porn found in junk shops. I wonder about my junk shop porn's provenance. Was the viewer just bored? Relieved to be rid of it? Or was the material taken there by a lover or close friend of someone who had recently died? Why was it sold on and not simply binned? I doubt there was much money in it. Whatever the reason, I thank those who kept the material in circulation; I thank as well all manner of sociologists, ethnologists, academics, book cover designers, collectors and curators for this wealth of material. I thank them for all the dirty bits found, rescued and brought to my attention. I thank all those who have celebrated porn and those who have condemned it. All who have led me to seek it out, the dodgy, dubious and sometimes ruthless industry included. A "special thanks" to the actors. I watch

If you look at it long enough...

you, you can't see me. I can be, and look, a total mess whilst watching you. Relax in your company. You won't know what I'm thinking. Nor will anyone else. I've switched off the phone, I can ignore the e-mails, mostly I will have locked the door, made certain that no-one is around. *Gentlemen, I address you privately; gentlemen I watch you privately. Gentlemen, I thank you publicly.* ¶But I'm never precisely sure who or what you are, and what pornography is. A few porn pics from my own life might shed some light, but then again, they might entirely confuse the issue. ¶To watch pornography is perhaps to disrupt time, to play with memory and to look forward to scenarios unlikely to happen. It rarely just simply takes me back, as does, say, a photo album. My relationship with porn favourites has lasted as long as, if not longer than, love, and as long as my most valued friendships. A lover wanted me to get rid of the sizable collection. Instead I hid it. He was jealous, for me to look at a magazine or a porn video was seen as kind of betrayal, unfaithfulness, a lack of attention to our relation, to him. When the relationship broke up (or rather changed to a different relation) the porn was there to return to. It came out of the cupboard, back in the open. I was once again on my own. Living on your own, you can leave the magazines around, return to them. There might be the dilemma – hide or show – when family or friends visit, or when the repairman calls (a classic role, the repairman, in many a porn scene scenario), but with the repairman the porn can come out of hiding in a kind of hope/fantasy that it might trigger action. Living alone, porn can be there for more relaxed viewing, not just looked at in the time it takes to wank (followed by its swift return to the hiding-place). You can develop a friendlier relation with the porn images. An altogether more drawn-out day-to-day affair. An affair that allows for accident/ incident with whoever might (but probably won't) enter your flat. And if a stranger does come, it's unlikely that he will fulfil the fantasy repairman role.

If you look at it long enough...

Repair or reparation. The fantasy figure at least provides some small compensation for all the things that went wrong with the more "ordinary" relations, family, best friends and lovers included. ¶Self-abuse is an extraordinary mix of fictional plays. The fantasies, triggered by porn, so often included the lover both before and after the break-up. In looking at porn I'm looking for reminders/

remainders of sexual encounters; there's a nostalgia to the looking. I'm astonished how, even in mass-produced porn I find a trace of someone met, a one-night stand, a childhood sexual experience, a longer-term lover. Older porn takes me back to haircuts and pullovers and wallpapers past. And, always, it reminds me of age and death. Boys from the Seventies, some will be dead now, of course. The haircuts oddly the most off-putting feature, but given the right face and body, I can mentally crop the hair, cut it "short back and sides." I can play with the image like a doll I might dress. It's as hard to describe the porn experience as it is to describe a dream. Collectors are notorious for their obsessive focus on particular acts, particular moments, repetitions and variations on them. For me the relation with porn is more like an exploration of the "what if?" The possible but unlikely relations, playful in a way that reality seldom is. I can watch almost anything "adult." "Scat" perhaps excepted. But "scat" too I've watched with a kind of fascination, even a kind of concern. Misplaced concern maybe, the "scat" boys certainly appeared to be enjoying themselves. ¶First there was Pete, aged nine, a rapidly maturing friend. Pete's brother had a drawerful of the stuff. Porn, run off a Roneo machine, stories in lilac ink. I remember a rape in a railway carriage. A woman alone, alone that is until three men joined her. There was no corridor for her to escape to. Trapped between stops. We would take the story, should Pete's parents be out at the pub, to Pete's bedroom to read it. "What do men do to women?" Pete would ask. I had no clue. We improvised on the theme, a mimicry of adult behaviour based on porn. It led to my first oral sex (I didn't think much of it at the time). It introduced me to the importance of nipples. To this day, if we play, I want your exposed chest as much as your cock. Well, with Pete I got to play "the woman," and fiction turned into to a different kind of fact/act. I've never understood the argument that pornography doesn't trigger action. It might not be a predictable or an immediate action. I have never been involved in a rape scene, or rather, I have never tried to rape. I did watch a girl once, Avril, have her small breasts exposed by Pete. I remember the unbuttoning of her blouse. It went no further. I was part of our small street gang (boys only) watching. I wanted it to go further, but only so that I could see more of Pete. I remember endlessly re-reading bits of the Bond novels, around that time. Bond's shirt seemed forever to be unbuttoned by the girls. Pete was my Bond. Or perhaps I've confused him with Sean Connery, that handsome face and hairy chest in the films. Pete was "mature" for his age, but not that mature. I wasn't entirely happy with my casting in Pete's porn-based scenarios, but it seemed, at the time, worth the compromise. Pete needed the excuse note of porn and a sex education/teaching role. I knew what I wanted: Pete. Pete is now part of my porn collection, though I have no photograph. And, if truth be told, so is Avril. Her firm breasts, small and sweet. It's only memory, imprecise memory, yet with many a detail. It's strange that I remember him, and remember her so often whilst watching porn tapes, forty years on. ¶He isn't a nine year old boy. I'm not having sex with a nine year old. He has grown, perhaps his shape relates to the "adult material" I'm watching now in some strange way. He is a "type" that is endlessly reproduced. The "boy next door" category in porn catalogue promotions. Though the boy next door is probably married and in a room where the fittings and furnishings, the textiles and the bed, are chosen by his wife. Much more sexy for me than the jock/ locker room scenarios. I've yet to see this porn film, men against a backdrop of flounce, chosen by women. A chest against a purple or a pink sheet, floral wallpaper. If you have come across the tape, let me know... ¶Rewriting Pete, re-envisaging him. Adding porn memories to "real" ones. I've met the odd boy next door, or two, in my time. The porn based relation leading to a kind of imagined relation. What would it be like to be with the boy next door? Or with the girl next door, or to be, perhaps, a part of their relation? To play "Uncle Paul"? I await the porn script commission. ¶I was once locked in a classically dank basement, I thought I might never get out, not unless I submitted.

```
Z$=+?~,::,,............?$+?I??I?==~=............,,,,:?DNDN?I:::~IIII777?77I???+?+=?II??+=.$$$$ZIZ
:::::,,/~,......I7$$Z++=~:7=+=?$:................:ONNNNNDND8+?$???++I??&77I???++==DD8??+==,Z$?Z=~+
,:~=::,,.......$D8Z+~~~==+=+=~:?E7?D?77..,::::::+NNNN8DOI$8Z77?++?Z$$N=77+!?+=++NDDD?+==+~77$8OOOO
+I+??=+?????I7I+?$8O?~:~=++!++=?ZZZZOZZ$O+$$$$$$$XMMDD8I?IXI$7I+?7888DZ=????Z=+HNNNI??++D7OO8O8
$8777$$77777I$7$$?+=~::=+??+=2OZOO8DO87I7$7$?8MN?I???I7II77DNNNN88?=??+?:?DDN8I??==88$888D88O
I$$$8777775$ZZZZOO?+=+!~=?!==::+OOOO8O8D8D8888ONO77?++?IINNNNNNN88Z=g=???~NDDI???+O7I88D8Z$
7Z$$778ZZZZZOZOO?+=~:,~==~~~=~O8O7OOO88DDN8OOZ$$$$I?IION877MNNNOI=g=????7ND8??I?OZO8D888DI
Z$$$$ZZZZOOOO0+++=~:,,==~=+8OOO$Z8888DDND8Z77II???I$$MNND7?IZO$I=g+?II??IN8???+8O$NDDDD8DO$
Z$ZZOOO2OO77I?+===~~:?+??!===~~OD8OZ88DDD8T$$II????+??IDNNMNN$7I7g==~,,:III?II?I78$OZDNDD$Z$
ZZZ$$ZO8$Z8OO++=:,:,,::~=%==~===~~O8NZDD8DZ77777?+?+++?=+?I7MMNMMD7I=g~,,=I7+?I?8OOZ=+8DDN8$$ZZ
Z2$$ZZZ8ZOOZO?+~,::~+=~:?+=:=8DODNND$I7II?++==+II++?I8NDNNNNI?=g!:~~=?88OZZZO$7DNNOOZZ
$ZZ$$$$$O8?ZO+=~:::~++==:?I7=m~??+DNDZIIII??+=~:+EO?====7NMMMMNI?+g~:.~77I$8D8OZZZZ$7NNNNOZ
$$$$OONZ$$NI++=~:~~=+?==~:~~:I?7D+==~:I77D+==~=IS$O8ZOZOg=DDDDD88OOOOO7INNND88Z
$$$$ZZDOOO8M7++=====?++++I?? =IN7II?+=~+++??I??+=~II$ZNE+=+/DOO88O8g~,~DDDD8D8O8OO77NNNDD88$
$I$ZOOOONONN+=:~~~=I+====~~=+NDDD7?+=+++~~~7$$DDO8Zg=O8OOOOZOZg~+8DD888OO8ZO$$INND88Z$
$$ZOOOZZN8DN?=~~~=?+~~=====~~+ONNDNMM$7I??+?~=~,~:=+IS=m77???++7OOg~=Z8DND888N7+++++?O8O8OZ$
ZOOZ$ZDDDDDNN=~~=I+=~:~=~~=?7OMNNNNI??+=~=+?+::?:~====$$$????I$OI=g+IS$Z88OOZ$$Z7+==+++?I8O$
ZOOZ8OOOO2O8NO=~~~~=O7?::::~~=,4?8DDDN7==?=~:,~=I+++?,,,,:~ZZ+?I$??I+g?IZOODOO88DDOOOOO7IOO8O$
ZZZZ2OOOO2O8ZZ?~:~~OZI=:::~~+?DDNI==~~?$=:,/:~~Z$=I?I?I7I=g++++$DD88OOOOOOZZZZZ8$
OOZZZZOOO88DZZO~+~:~OO$+=~,,,,:+IZND?==+I7I+==++7=:~~~=I??I$II7ZZ$=g??II??+=~8OZZZZZZZZZZO8
ODZO88OOOOODZO=~+~:?$ONI+=~7+4$7III==g???III+==++7?7??7I$7Ig=II?I?~+=~88DOOOOOOD
N8ZZEZOOOODN88?~~~+8$+~~=::~~OO$=:,,,,~??IZ$+?II7+++IMg$88Z$$Z8??+??I7I??I?7=g??7+++=~+DDDDDNNNNNDOO
NOZEO88D88888OO7~~==+DD$I?+=:~?I77I7Z7?+=~/8Z$88OOO8??I$???I(876=g???????++==~OOOOOOZZOZ$
NEZZZZZ2OZZZ$Z$=m==+ZZZI++=~::~+I7ZZZ$I+++=IM$88DZZ$EZ8I+++IDD77?I+?877++?=+ZZO88880ZZ$$77
OOZZZEZOO8ZOOZ$I++=====O888O+~,:~770$$Z~?788DO$8888OOZZZZDO???O?$7I?+?II=g~~ZOOO88Z$Z$
ZZZZOOOOOO80Z$$$$===08880+:,:~-77$$$??7888OO$$ZOI??O???8?$7I?+?I?=g~~ZOOO888OZ$
$$ZZEZEZOZOZOZ$$Z7+==+8808=:,:-~77$$$7?7788800$$ZOI??I?=+++78IIII?=g~~~77$8$+-DI???=OZO8O8OZZ
IIDZZZZZOZZOO8ZO88+?==O8D=:::-=I$g777$DDD8OZ8OO8I??$ON?+=+I7777II7?g??+=7$+-I?++?$OODD88O
888ZZZZZZ$8D8D888+==+?778$=::==I8g7?788DOZ$ZZZN77?+?~$NNNNI=?OI7$77I?g?++=7$??++=?I708OOO888DD8
8D$ZEO7?78NNND$I??+===+?III=::-~NO8ZZZ$ODDO8OODDI??IZDDMN$I7771~:?g:?????+=-I7iI88888OO88888
DII7??~~~~77??+====?==+?7II+:=~-MN8O7II7Z78O$7I$$$I7$T$7ZO87Z7$gMMN7$?~.~$=+??+:,::,::,,,,
?I?+?~~=+??I$$ZO$7??=7I7$$+:~==-MN8O7I?7Z78O$7I$$$I7$7$ZO8Z7T7$gMMN7$7?~.~$=+??+::::~,,,
??=~~~~==?=+==+++?=++=?I+I$7ZN?~===-8NNMN8I?!==i8NNMNNI=?OI7$77?=T7gMM77++?????9??+ZII+,,:~:,,,
$+=+!~==ODDI77++?+=~~~::~i=$+=~~-+8NMM8$7?:==NNME7MO77OM$I7II71I7I7I$g7=+?+??????9?+ZII+,,,:~:,
888~O=I7??+?NNNND7?I?++====~~~-7MMNO?$++?:=~NMDI7++?+?++II==~?+++g+T7$??II?7I?II?I?I??ZNDZ:I
Z?=ID7ONDDMD+?$$DMNNNN+==#?~+-$$$DMS7I$8N=~,$Z7====+=++7?+=+++??I?I7IZ7II7??????II7I75+:D
8OO8ONZ?=$ZOMN7?$D7+~NN$77+D7+~==MI++~+=MMI++++?+++??I2I4+????I7II77OZIZI???????????IIDD
=Z~:I?OMMND0?,D8?:~~=8DDID$DIE78NDD8I7ZE+~+OSI?7++=~=+=+++$$$$Z8DDDNNNN$$O8D$7I?I?????????II?IN
~::I8OZOOO=:,,7~==~?$==+=ZI?8Z=??7DD8DDI7I+++IMZ7I?+?+++??+==++?+?IIZN?+?INNNDDD$77$7III????+?+I7+I
```

Apologies for the following unsexy and unpromising scenario. We met in an ornate Victorian-style, mirrored pub. I had my ticket to the opera and was determined not to miss it. We agreed to meet later, near his home, by a tube station in a smart part of London. To my surprise he turned up. He took me to a flat with metal bars on the windows. He locked the door. I had no choice really, and this, I quickly realised, was a major mistake. I hope you are imagining the scene, and enjoying it, and adding your own memories and fantasies. I didn't enjoy it at the time. Revised recollections have failed to transfigure it. I could give you more detail, the room, dark and fetid, with hideous wallpaper. You might like that. Or I could transform it into a glossy and glamourous scenario. I could let you pick and choose from the available options you have seen and read so many times before. Add or subtract the detail that makes it work for you. Delete all reference to "opera" for example. Closer. Was he wearing the cleanest of briefs, or baggy boxers, stained? If I add that he was handsome and smooth, or that he was handsome and hairy-chested, would it ruin the fantasy or make it more ornate? Would you prefer ugly and rough? Can you avoid certain words and add your own memories to the scene? Does the cock-size matter? I have no memory of his cock, only that I had to take it, as quickly as possible, in order, I hoped, to be allowed out. ¶I could tell you too about a different lover, an earlier one, one who loved porn. That was a more "open" relation. I wasn't jealous of his affairs and adventures, I was envious. I wanted to be a part of them. He went out one evening. Just cruising. The man who picked him up took him back to a flat. Others lay in wait. They tied him up. A gang-bang. That scenario I did manage to transform, in spite of the damage that was done to him. The porn fantasy seemed to make the reality of a messy, painful and hideous experience easier for the lover to deal with. It also helped me. He admitted that in retrospect, once he was over the nervous shake and the pain, it seemed like a sexy thing to have happened. I could read from the book or show you the film version of Selby's *Last Exit to Brooklyn*, complete with searing music, and remind you of the rag-doll character, Tralala, gang-banged, a bottle pushed into her. Tralala abandoned and finally done with. To have done with. To be done with. I could transform *Last Exit* into a gay scenario, though I suspect the scene was sexy enough for gay men anyway, with its men, in turn, unbuttoning. A guilt, perhaps, at reading/seeing the rape, but a sexiness tinged with sorrow. Another function of porn. To get rid of the

```
7771?I77II??II?III77II?III7IIII7777I7877I?I77II??IIIIII77II??I?I?II??I????????IIIIIII77III7
787777II?III??II??I?I???I?I$$I77777787787777IIIII??I?I????I?I???????????I??????????I??I??I??
I7IIIIIIII??II?II???II?I778777777I77IIIIIIIII??II?II????IIII?I????????I??????????I??I??I??
$778$87$78$8$Z$$ZO$ZZO88OOZZ$Z$$$$7771?7IIIII???I?I?I?IIIII???I?I?III??I????????I?????????
I8$6ZO888OZ$ZOOOZZZ$$$$ZOZ8$$$7778$ZE$777777777II?IIIIIII?III?I77IIIIIIII??I?????????I?????
ZZO8888BOOOOOO8BOZOEZO8DD8DO$$77$6ZE$I787777II78$$7?78$78$777777II77778$6777IIII????????I??II?I
$ZO88OOZZZZZ$$Z$Z88NMMMMNNNMO$777$$8ZI7IIII??I??I?7II78OOO8O$7IIIIIIIIIIIIIIIIIII7IIIIIIIII
777778$$787$778$778MNDNNDNMMMMMZZM878777787$87$$$$$$$$ZEOO88BOOO8OOoooo8$77II78$ZZEZ$77IIIIIIIIIII77
777777777777778DMMMMMMDDNMMMMDZ$MMO77777778$ZZZ$$$$$$$ZOOZ$8$887788$$$$$ZOEZEZEZOEOOOOO$$7
7777777777771MMMO8DDD8DNNNBO8Z$DNO77777II7777I7II7777777777777IIIII78?777778$7787$77II
7777777777I77ZMNMMB8DM8OZZ$Z$ZOOZODD8777771?77II77778$7777878IIII71IIIIIIIIIIIII77III7777777
ZZ$$$$$$$777$NNDDMOM8O88ZZ$$8777I7777788II777ILZ$777IIIIIII7777777777788$7777IIIIIII7II7IIIII
$$$$87$6$778$8NDB8NN8NDZ$ZZZZZ$Z$7IIII77?ZOZZ$87777??IIIIII7IIIIII77777I7777IIIIII77IIIIIIII
ZZZ$Z$$$7$Z77DMMMOD8D8ZZZZZZ$ZOOZOZ$778$$$71?$OOOZ77I77IIIIIIIIIIIIIIIIIIIIIIIIIIIIII7IIIII
$78$$$$$ZZZ$$7MODDDNNOOZZZZ$$778$OOOZ$$$$$$$ZE$7III7I8$7II7I?III7IIIII7IIIIIIIIIIIIIIIIIIIIIII
777777$6$$7770$7ZMDOZZ$$Z$$77Z8OOOZZ$87$ZZZ$$7I??77III?III7779II7I7I7IIIIIIIIIIIIIIIIIII7IIIIII
76787777777$7$$ON77MNZZZZ$$7772D88OOOOZ$$$ZZZ$7I??$71??IIII?78$76I787I?7II77?I777777IIII7III7I77I7I
77778$78$78$77ZMN$7OOZ$$Z$$7I78ND88OOZZZZZZZ$7+I$877????77I7I778$$I$6$$$I777III??I?I?I7II777III7?
$$$$$$$$$$7$7778ZE7777$$ZZ$$$71I7MNDD8OOOZOZZZZEZZ$7I$$$771??IIZ$I7I7I777779I7ZES$E$67ES$7+7777771771
77777777777777777778$ZE$$$$$71$8MMN88BOOOOOOZZ$$$$ZZE$$87II?777I7IZEZEEZOOOOZ$$67$7777778?777878767777
77777777777777777778$ZE$$$$71$8MMN88BOOOOOOZZ$$$$Z$$$87III?78$7777IIII77III777777II7777777IIII
877777777777777777Z0OZ$$$$ZDDNNNND8BOOOOZZZZ$$$Z$$$$771II7877777777777777777I777777777II
$$ZZZ$$$$$$$$$$$O8OOOOZZZZ$DDNDND8BOOOOOOZZZEZ$$$ZZZZ$$$7711$$$$$$$$$$$$$$$$$$$$$$$$$$$$$
$$$$$$$$$$$$$$$Z$88888OOO8$$$8DD8BOOOOOOOOZZZES$$ZZ$$$777III?0I$$$$$$$$$$$$$$$$$$$$$$$$$$$$
$$$$$$$$$$$$$$$8888OOO$$$8OO8DD8BOOOOOOOOOOOZ$67I$$$$7I777II$$$$$$$$$$$$$$$$$$$$$$$$$$$$$$
$$$$$$$$$7$$$$$$888888877777O8888BOOOZEZZZZE6$677777I?777777777777IIII77788?78?77777777777$$
$$$778$$$$$7777788888888877777788888OZ$7777777I7777III??+?77777777777777777787877777777$$
78678$778$778$78888888888$$$7O$877$77777IIII?777777II??II?7777777777777777777787877777777777
$$87777778$77778$7088888888877777$Z$$$$$$8$777777I?8$877777IIII?+77777777807877777877777777777777
77777777$$78$78$Z8D88888887$77ZZ$$$$$$$$$$777$$$$$$$$77I?I7777777IIII?+77777777877777777777777$
$778787678777777$D8DDDDDD777ZZZZZ$Z$$$$$$$$77$ZZZ$$$$$87I7I??I77777777867777777777777888$77
78$77777$77777$778DDDDDD8777ZZZZZ$ZZ$Z$$$$$$$ZZZZ$$$$$787777I??I77777777778777777777777777787
778$77777777777777$8DDDDD8777ZZZZZZZZ$Z$$$$$$ZZ$$$$$$$8777711??77777777777777777777867777777
Z$6$87777778Z$6ZE$88DDDD8Z$77ZZZZZZZZZZZZZZZ$$$$$$$$$$ZE$7I8$$$$$$$$7777777777777777777678$7
78$77777777777777$08DDNNO$OZZ$ZOZZZZZZZEZZZZOOZZZZEZ$$$$$$$$$$$$$$$$71777777777777787$$$$7787
7777777777777777708DNNNOOOOOOOOOZZZZOZZZZZZZZZ0B8OOZZZZZZZZZZZZZ$ZE$$I?I77777777777777777
787777777777777777O8DDZZZEOBOOOOOOOOOOOOZZZZEO8DO8OOZZZZZZZZZZZOZZE$7III??I77788$7777878777$
78$78777778777$7Z8OZZZZZOOOOOO8OOO8OOOOOO8ZZ00DNOOOOOZZZZ$ZE$7III??78$777777778777777777
7767777$$ZO$$ZO$$ZZZZ0008888888BOOOOOO8DNNB800000000000ZZ$771I?7II??I$67777077$77777777$$
7E$$$$$$OZZZOOZZZZOOOO000888888888888O8OO8DDNBOOOOOOORO00000000ZE$77777777I777777II777777777$$
ZZE$$$$$$$$ZZOOOOOOOOOOOO00888888888888BDDDD888B88DDDLOB88888888OOOZZ$$$$$$6Z$$677777777788$777
$$$$$$$ZZE7$$OOO888888OOO8888888888888BDDDD8888DDLOB88888888OOOZZ$$$$$$6Z$$$$77778$777$$7$7
$8ZO$$$ZZZZ8NDDD88888888888DDDDNMNDDDDDD$?OMNN     NNN7I$8D8DDD8888BDDDD8888O0OO88087$77I177$$87$$7$7
ZO$$$ZZZOZOZOO8DMMMDDDDDDDDNNNMMMMMMDDO??IMMNN     NN7I$77+ZDDNNNMMMMNN$ZO8$I?IIIII7$$$$Z$$7$$7
ZZO8OZOOOZZZZOO8DMMMMMNNNMNNMMMNNNNI?II?INNNML     NN8I$777+ZDDNNNMMMMNN$ZO8$I?IIIII7$$$$Z$$7$7$I$7
8DZZZOOOZZZZE$Z$7NMMMMMMMMMMMNDMDD7IIIIIIIINNDD    DDD777E????DNNMMMNNOOOOO27I$$$$78ZZZ$$7777$7
NNNNDN8B8OOO8$O08OOOOMMMMMMMMMNZ$77DB777777777IND    ND$7777I7I187I2NDN8BO8888BOI$ZZEOOOOO$$$87
MM8DZ888O07O088888OOO8MMMMMMMMMO8E$$$DO808$7777I6N    NM7777$87778$788O88BOO8BO7=OO0$87$$$$
NDDD8DD77OO88888888OOMMMMMMMMBOOOZND8888Z$$$777$    ZZZZZZZ$$Z$$ZZZD8888888888O$I+8OOOZ$$$$$Z$
888O$ZZOOO8D888888BMMMMMMMMMD08B8N8DDOZ$ZZZEZ$   8OZZZZ$$ZZZZZZO8DNDDDDD8888OOO8OZIO08$$$$$$$
88$ZZOZZOZOO888$8DMMMMMMMMMOZZOZZOO$$$$$$$$$$$   8O$ZZZZZZZZZO8MD88BNMBDDDB8888O0T=NDB$$$$$$$$
ZOZZZZOOZOOOD8DD8MMMMMNMMMMMMMNZ$$ZZZ$6$Z$787$  7$OS$$$$$$ZZZ$7ZZOOOOOOOOO8MMMBB8OOO8B8OOZI8O8$$78$$$
OOZZZZZZZ$$6$8DDMMMMMMMMMMMMMMZ$$$$$8I7$787787$ 78$$8O$$ZZZZZZZ$$ZZ$$$ZZEOMMMMMNNOOO8B8OO7O8E$$$$$$
OZE$Z$$$$OOO8DNDNDNNDNDNNNDDDNMNMMMO777Z7$78$Z DND$ZZZZ$$Z$Z$$$$$Z8MMNNNNNOOOZZOO8ZZOOZZE$$
OOOZ$$ZZZZO8DNMMNDNND8DD88$DDNNDNMMO77I77III7$7$$Z6NDD7$7$$78$7$778$ZMMMNNDDDB8DOOZZOOOOOOO7$Z$
8OOZZZZZOOODNDMDD8D8DD888$DD88BDDNMZ77777I78$$$8$ZE  DNOO$$78$$78$7777ZNNDD8D8OB88OOOOO88OD8$$$$
88ZZ$ZZZZN88880008888$8O8DDNMDDDDDDBDDDNMZ77777$78$$$  DNOO$7$6$787777I7$I$7187I78NND888B88OZOOOOOOO88BZ8O$$$$$
D8D888NZ88OOD88ZO88O8OOOOO800888O888NMZ7I7II7I777ZEEIII7I7I7II77$I$NN8D88O88OOOOOOOO888888O88$$$$$
D8O888OOO888BNDOOOOZOOOOZO0Z0O8DMMMMMMM8$7$ES$$$717$ZZ$$$7I$I78MMN800OOOO8Z00O88ND8D88DO8OZD8$7$$$
D8DDON8ODDN8BOOO8O8ZEZOZZOOOOZODMDMMMMMM8$77III778IIIII7I7ZNDB0OOOZZOO8OOZOOOOOZOOOZZZ$$$8O8ZZ$8Z$$$$$$$
8OOOOOOZZZZZZZ$$$ZZOZ8D8NMBNNMMMMMMMMMDBNMMD8BOO8ZZZZZE8NDOOOOOZOZZZZZZZOZZZZZZ$$$ZZ76$$$$O$$
ZODDDN8OOZOZZ88888DO$ZDMMMMN888ZOZOZZZZZZ$ZZZZZZZZ$$$ZZZ$$$ZZZZZ$$$ZZEZ$$$Z$Z$$$$7$$$$$$$$$$
```

painful memory, play with it, transfigure it. ¶Porn as part of the history of every room I've ever lived in, and I've lived in many. Every window that I've regularly and repeatedly looked out from. Often transfixed and reluctant to move from the desk, always placed with an eye to the view. Every room with a stash of porn under the bed. The fantasies so often combine the view with the hidden material, the private collection. The self-abuse draws them inexorably into one dream-like picture, a picture I only need to possess for the time it takes to cum, probably longer than I might spend in front of a "great" painting in a gallery. Porn: your very own porn picture gallery, one that permits you to slip and slide between images. It needs no museum, no home, no walls, and little money. Not even a picture hook, nails and a hammer. Cheap pictures, easily acquired. Landscapes/ladscapes. The images you create watching porn would be almost impossible to reproduce. You can't sell them, share them, make a print of them or pass them on. The images

If you look at it long enough...

you create might be blurred, awkward and imperfect, but they are, perhaps, beyond value. It is astonishing how fantasies, unless interrupted by the day-to-day ("Did I switch that iron off?") forever give satisfaction, how they seem for that moment, just right. And no-one is around to bother you, as they are in the gallery. No irritating voices, no security guard, no gift shop seller. All of them miraculously disappear from the scene. You don't need to buy a catalogue, though you might have created a rough and ready one, a cheap one of your own. Even that is a catalogue you are unlikely to cling to. You will let it fall from your hands as the perfect relation with the image, the perfect moment, arrives. And you can replace and replenish your hand-made catalogue, create your own "private view," complete with drinks and whatever else might assist the pleasure. You need no fully annotated and referenced guide. You have picked and mixed a hundred images, and there is no academic requirement to cite your sources. No need for a list of illustrations starting with Fig. 1. ¶Is pornography any different to voyeurism? Revisiting the walks, often carefully taken. Always passing that window, on that side of the road, at that time of the day when the time is right, when that building site is, weather depending, in full and shirtless progress. Or that chanced on, once only moment, forever remembered. I get to edit of course, and I'm not trying to attract another viewer. I'm not trying to make money out of the man, or out of the home movie running in my head. But the repeat, that man with the child on his shoulders, seen from the back, close, tight hair. Tattoos, but small, discreet almost. Walking in front of him, pretending to be watching the Red Devil Air Display, red, blue and white spray in the sky, a striped smoke. He keeps coming back to me. He entered my diary and my private porn collection. Remembering him, a regret now for that brief and silent pleasure on an otherwise dull day. Few published diary entries record so many acutely important – at the time – fleeting encounters.

If you look at it long enough...

The men the writer deliberately watched for hours or quickly walked past, day after day. Walks and windows, forever staring, hoping that if I look at it long enough... ¶Is it just a fixation, wank fodder? Is it trying to tease out something more, something new? Is it adding to experience or erasing it? It is certainly irresponsible, or perhaps an avoidance of responsibility. An avoidance of relation, a sin in so many eyes. Call me irresponsible, call me unreliable. Call me a wanker. ¶*Another explanation for the artist's fragility is, paradoxically, the resoluteness and the insistence of his gaze. Power, of whatever form, because it is violence, never gazes; if I were to gaze a minute more (a minute too long), it would lose its essence as power. He, the artist, pauses and gazes slowly, and I can imagine that you became a filmmaker because the camera is an eye, that is, constrained by its technical nature to gaze. What you add, as do all great filmmakers, is to gaze at things radically, to the point of exhausting them. ... This is dangerous, because gazing at something*

If you look at it long enough...

far longer that you were asked to (I insist on this supplement of intensity) upsets the established order in whatever form, since the extent or the very duration of the gaze is normally controlled by society. Whence – if the work escapes this control – the scandalous nature of certain photographs and certain films, not the most indecent or the most aggressive ones, but merely the ones that are the most "posed."[1] ¶Perhaps it is too grand a claim for pornography. But then again, surely the authorities are worried about something else in pornography, something other than the preservation of family values, the protection of women, the exploitation of children. Something beyond the easy complaint. Trotted out equally often, another compliant. Porn is a rip-off industry. Often, but not always (there are "one-off" and individual home-made amateur tapes), the makers want you to look at the tape again, to trust their product and yet to persuade you, often with teasers/trailers, to purchase another. The next tape in the series or all of the tapes featuring one of

1. Barthes, R. (1989), "Dear Antonioni," In S. Chatman & G. Fink (Eds.), *L'avventura: Michelangelo Antonioni, director*. (p. 212). New Brunswick, NJ: Rutgers University Press.

their models. Much the same goes for many a consumer product, of course. It can't be the commercial exploitation that so offends porn's detractors. Note their silence and indifference when punters, should they pluck up the courage, report porn and peep show rip-offs, or even when they die in porn cinema blazes. What is it then that so bothers them, even in consenting gay male and adult porn? Could it be that the porn viewer squanders time? That the pornography plays with time? An illusion of real time, but with the edit, the repetitions of the notorious "cum shot" in particular, the pornographer hooks the viewer, plays with them, makes them play with themselves. The sheer sterile waste of it all. Perhaps to squander time is, after all, a kind of resistance. ¶To look forward to scenarios unlikely to happen. And to look back on and revise your relations. Even relations with old porn favourites. So many tapes I've watched repeatedly have finally jammed in the video player, or, if bought cheaply, their colours have slowly dissolved. Then the frustration.

If you look at it long enough...

Can you find another copy of that particular "Russian Soldier" tape when you need it? New titles only in stock. Just as with favourite books, favourite films, you revise your relations with old porn, the porn you keep, the porn that survives. You might find that certain images no longer work. And yet you hang on to them. Much as you might keep a photo of an ex-lover, one perhaps that you were once physically obsessed by. The look of the lover changes, of course, if you keep in touch, if you see him over the years. The porn image remains the same. New porn models arrive; new tapes. The porn "model" looks remain, the contemporary "ideal" changes. New styles, new haircuts and clothes, new markets, new openings for boys from new countries. Fresh to-be-desired images. The old ones, though you might retain an affection for them, seem seriously past their sell-by or their imaginary shag-by-date. To be stashed away, perhaps to make a rare reappearance, an eventual comeback. If you calculate the age and condition of the

old model now, it could be off-putting.
¶As I get older I find that I want increasingly to detach myself from the business of "present" sex. I don't go out with the intention of finding it, or even a lover, anywhere near as often as I used to. In some ways I prefer my adventures second-hand, pornographic ones created for me (and thousands of others). Or I might prefer an internet connection. Tell me your story, show me your image. Send it, addressed to me, electronically or privately in the post and under "plain cover." I don't really want to join my dated German video suburban bisexual orgy, but I might enjoy observing it. On tape, on the Net, or in the flesh. Any which way really. To observe action, to not be a part of it. To delete myself, even from the fantasy scenarios. I never felt totally outside of porn before. It was always me looking for that be-shorted boy in that tree, a picture kept for years. Me that converted the UK law-required soft core into something altogether more hard and harsh. I have abused myself with so many boys, times, places, texts

If you look at it long enough...

and images, all to the accompaniment of a vast range of music (from the tape or, volume turned down low, from my own music collection). I've been aided and abetted by all manner of toys, ointments and apparatus. I've found comfort and consolation in courtroom dramas, old documents. The clinically reported sodomitical acts, from the eighteenth century to the present. Imagined the circumstances and acts that led to the imprisonment, and even to the death of the participants. The changing shape of my desires, from the rare and snatched images found in the 1960s, mostly American physique mags, to the occasional English boy next door. Now it tends to be the boy next country or next continent. The Web assists the search. Thank you, Google. Porn from the Arab world, from North Africa, often produced in France. Marseille now my fantasy city. A porn World Cup. The cup filleth and the cup runneth over. Is that the phrase? ¶Pictures of miners, pictures of sailors, pictures of footballers, they're still in my collection, mixed with memories of those older fantasies, the boy next door, even a football player brother-in-law. I can create inter-racial scenarios, mix images of people met, the cute but scarred, the damaged and the drugfuct boys in clubs included. Added

```
8Z8O$DNODOND788$DD8DD8DZN8D8Z$$$78ZI77$ZOI7I$ZI8$I?I?II$$$$I$IZ$IO?O77II$I8O7Z7I7IIII777777777$$$$O
DNND$8N$D8ZDZ8D$88ZDDZO$Z8ON8ZOIZO8DIDDN8I$OZ8I8$I????I$$$$I$IZ$I$I8I7II7IDO7$7I7IIII7777$77777$$$
DD$DZNO$DN$ODO8$ZOZOO8O$OZ8ZZZ?.7$D7NN8D7$D7Z$$7II?I?I$7$$?$7$$I$IO7$II7I8Z7$II7IIII77$$77$$ZO
DO7DM$88DN$$DIN8ODZ78MMMNMMMMD7ZO7NINDZN$IZIZ$8D?I?I?I$7$$?$$$$IZIO77II7I8$77II7IIII7$$$77$77$$OZO
O8$N8?DNZ7$ND7ZD8DOMMDMNNMMNMMDZ$DOM$NN7MZ7O7808DI??I?I7$$$IZZ7ZIZIO77II7I88I7II7IIII7$$$$78$77$$$O
7OZ8$$NN78DNN$8D$NNMDMMNNNMMMM$IODMNDNM7NO$$Z$77II??7II777ZIZZIZIZ$O77IIII8ZI$II7IIII77$$$$$$$7$$770
Z88$O$MN$DN8D888$DMMNN8M8N?INO?II$MMN$DON8$7OD8788??7?II77Z7$ZZIZ7$8$7I7I77OOI$II7IIII7$$$78$$7$$70
ZD8$ZMZD8NM$DNNN$NNNMMMDNNII++++??$DMM7DDND$ZO88ID$I?I?II77I78=7$I$Z$8$7I7708I$II7IIII7$77777777770
ZZD$78$NMND$O8$NZMNNN8ZNNO+$?=+??I78DIDNDD7DO7II$7I?IIII8I$78?I$ICOZ77I7I7$Z8I$II7II7777777777770
O$NOII$NMON$D8$DN8N8NN8$N8++==+??I$$8INO8NIM8$IIIIII??I$I?I$I?IIII7$7$I7I7Z$OI$II7II7777777$7777770
I$?=Z7$88$7I$8$NDDNNM8DN8O?=+==+??I$8TOZ$ZIOO$7IIIIIII78I777ZI$I7OIZI7I$770I$II7IIII7$$$7777ZZ$7770
+$$I$=I7$?+$:~+=O+MMMM8Z+==+?+?I$I$7$$DOD87I7IIIII$7$$78I7I$ZIZ777777$I9I77III7I$$$7777Z$$7770
???7III$7I7???$?7I7Z&+$NZI+===+2?II7777777777IZ77IIIII$$$Z7ZIZ77Z7777777$II77III$$8772OZZZZO
$+$++7=I=+$+??+$+?Z??7OI?+===+$IZ77777$7777I7I7I7I1$OZZIZ70MMMMMMZBM8MZ77$$7777$II7II$Z$ZZO
$+$+$?+7$++++$+++7?++?$Z8$7??I7Z76????III77IIII7777??$$$6OMMMMMMN8DNMNDN7$7$77$$I$II$ZOO$ZZZO
2$+====+++++++?=+??78$7$++===++?1?I7II$$$II7II$$8SI77I$$$$$$7$$$Z$I77$ZOO$$ZZZ$O
?+====+=$=+$+$?77O$Z7+++=+?$==-=-=+???I$7$77OC$DND8??7I7777808D8ZO$$OZ7??I7$ZO$$$$Z$O
?+=Z8=O+?=$$====+++?I77Z$$I?+++???7====++++$I77I$777OZ8$I777$8080ZZZ$$OZ77II7$ZO8O$$$O
?Z++7+=?==++++?I77$8D$I?+++????7=====-++?II7$$7777Q8IZ$$8O88$OOZZZZ$$O7$78ZZ77?7O
?+=====+I$$Z$$$$$$ZZ$77$ZOI?+???+?$+++====+++??I7I7$Z:-I$I8OIIII7ZO8OOZZZ8$I7$ZZ$77?70
I?++++?+++????7?I777777777?OOI?+++?+?Z8O8Z$7I??+===++??I7I7?7I7$080OZ$8$$$7$$OZ??7O
I??????IIIIIIIIII7777777777ZN$I?+++?$8888888O$II?+====++?I7$7II7I7?77+?=+?7ZOZOOO8D$777$OZ??I?O
ZOZ$77777777I777777IIIIIIIIIED$I?+??7IIIII288888888Z$7I??+++==-++III7I77??+?$+==+++O8OOZZZ$$$ZOII?IO
$$$ZZZZZZZZZ$7777II7IIIIIIIIO78777??IZ$7I78I$7I$I8IN$I++++===-++II$I$Z$77??7?O$ZZZ$$$ZOIIIIO
888B$$$$$$$$$7777777IIII???$78ZZ7II$8I?S7??I7I$Z$NZ$7II:::,,+$$77777778$$$ZZO?IIO
8DND88OOO8OD87777777I77I$O7?I7O$$87I$I??????7II7$D?~-===?,,,::~-~+7+4N$ZZZ$$$$ZOOI77I70
DDDD88D8888ON$7777777I7IIID77$IIO87I?$IO8?I7$I7?????ZZZ8$7IIII177DO:=-:~-~+$ZZ$$$$$ZOOI7I70
DDDD88NNDMMM$7777777777ZZ77IOO$I7B$$$8OZ$7777IIIII177$?????7ZI????7+=~+I=-====??+$$$ZZZ77777?8O
DDNNZZ8$$$$Z$7777777IZ78$77OZ$7OZ$ZZO$77III77$$Z$7?$$Z$$$$Z$71777$$$7II+=====+???$$$$$ZO7777II70
DD8$$$$$$ZZ$Z$$$77777ZZ$8$7777$Z$$OZ$Z8$787$Z$OZOOZZ$$77IIII777$7$$777$?7?=====++???IOZ$$$ZO$777$$$$O
OOOOOOOOOOOOOOOOOOOOOOOOOOOOOOOOOOOOOOOOOOOOOOOOOOOOOOOOOOOOOOOOOOOOOOOOOOOOOOOOOOOOOOOOOOOOOOOOOOO
```

to that, my witnessing of many a prostitute/client exchange, the show courtesy of a male prostitute friend. The watching was always with the client's consent, and seeming pleasure. I looked on, sometimes for hours. A privilege, a pleasure that returns, often as I'm watching an unrelated porn tape. A mad, shifting and joyous porn theatre in my head. ¶Nowadays I watch, not exactly detached, the porn performance. But I'm not that engaged either. In that I'm not unlike so many of the performers. I look for a degree of realism in the facial expression, the moments when the guard drops, when the pleasure seems unfaked. I'm fascinated by the clothes (and hate it when the film starts with the actors already near naked). I'm caught by the backdrops, the detail, the bedding, the landscape. Backdrops that I suspect often belong to the filmmaker. A curious relation of the actors to the set to the maker, rare in mainstream film. Rough boys in smart apartments. I enjoy the often clumsy relation of performer to the unfamiliar surroundings, unlikely objects. I love tapes with words, the awkward dia-logue. Sometimes the performer will introduce himself, to another performer, or direct to camera, to you the viewer. Often in a language I don't understand, or it's simply a verbally embarrassed performance, or the shoddy sound quality makes it impossible to hear. People complain at the lack of narrative in porn. Well, I welcome the trite repeated classic stories and scenarios; I can add sub-plots of my own. I realise that often, though I'm enjoying the view, the acts themselves no longer necessarily fascinate me, or even appeal. I watch far more straight porn than I used to, and it isn't just the men who excite me, but I'm not for the turning. ¶A fondness for the amateur, the "straight" man caught by the gay camera has retained its appeal. From John S. Barrington's 1950s and 1960s collections, under such titles as *The Male Nude in Fine Art* through to the much later and little known "Barbican Tapes." Cards were handed out by an antiques collector to boys in and around this exclusive City of London estate. They might model sportswear, swimwear, skateboard clothes. Paid modelling possibilities on offer. He caught a number of skateboarding boys on the expensive city estate, others were city boys. They came round, they might have been shown his razor collection. An alarming collection, to say the least. Blades from across the world. Don't ask me how I know. Most were shown his work, boys posed, as if for a collection of catalogue/mail-order clothes. Starting with sportswear. If they were interested, they could view a sample portfolio of men undressing. Catalogues, with varying degrees of the explicit. They might, if interested, care to look at the orgies. The videos were recorded for his own purposes, he assured them, unless they were interested in sales of stills to magazines. The tapes were circulated around London, an underground network of tape deliveries. Specialist, seemingly "straight" male pose stuff. Some stayed in swimwear, some wanked, some joined the circle jerks. Tapes passed on and sold for gay consumption. Real boys in real clothes undressing and then trying on his handy and cherished collection of menswear. My memory is hazy, and I had to return the borrowed tapes. I was sad to lose sight of them; they were sold on by the friend who suddenly wanted to rid himself of the addiction. I do have fragments of my notes on the tapes, a few words that bring back to life the not entirely handsome and elderly man, who kept leaving his camera on the tripod to give the boys a hand. I remember his posh and squeaky voice. And the Irish, I think, soft-spoken voice of the awkward model. Sadly the Irishman's words have long gone. *"Can you stand with your back to the light? ... black pants on ... do some muscle poses? ... fantastic ... yes ... slightly to the left ... Smile ... do a back view ..."* ¶Dozens did this, thousands do it. It seems that thousands of boys enjoy being photographed the world over. Thousands, I think, want a record of their bodies. Prime-time flesh on tape. I don't believe that the majority were either conned or desperate for the cash. I've seen the desperate ones – they're not hard to spot. Often there are marks on their arms, or signs in their eyes. From 1962 to 2002, from being 10 to reaching 50, I have looked. Starting with stories, through to downloaded video clips from the Net. I've only ever

(thanks to new technology) made one porn appearance myself. A man I was having sex with, unusually for me, in an alley, after meeting in a pub (turned out he had been at the funeral wake for a friend), asked if he could use his digital camera. I was startled and flattered; and I hope, a few years on, that he still enjoys the show. ¶Many a tape has broken, but I've kept most of my porn collection. Even when the bulk and burden seems heavy, even when, on rare occasions, I resolved to cut down, or even give up. Only one or two videos have been altered, a careful taping over any hint of child-sex. Usually just carefully shot swimming pool images, in ads for other tapes available from commercial gay porn companies of the 1970s and the 80s. They had to go. Adult abusive stuff, in all its theatricality, I've held on to. The supplement to the collection, clips taped from TV neatly labelled "News Clips" – highlights from dramas, but also from the news; documentaries transformed into "News Clips," not an entirely euphemistic device, for keeping the tapes from prying flatmates' eyes. I'm not alone in finding Israeli soldiers and their Palestinian prisoners sexy. News pics find their way onto many a porn site. Then there is the notebook I kept, the record of the male prostitute's activities, a list of codes and words to describe every act, and every price. Words enough to trigger the memories. Walls of academic books, many of them "Gay Studies." Diaries of my window watching days... ¶I seem to have taken to "solo" acts, to the solitaries now, I've abandoned the couples and the group sex tapes, or put them in cold storage. The current favourite is my collection of solo "beurs," the North African boys of Marseille. The boys undress, sometimes looking to camera as if to ask if they are doing what is required, doing what they're being paid for. Some look entirely off-screen, perhaps at a silent straight porn tape; to keep the interest up? Most seem distant from the task, though some clearly enjoy their own bodies, enjoy the display. A few of the boys even hold back, as they cum, on the final sigh. They won't allow you to think they're enjoying it. Why do I want to cum at the moment they do, especially the reluctant ones. Why do I enjoy their distance? I certainly relish their awkwardness in the striptease. And then the occasional spots, the "flaws" on their bodies, the scars and the cheap tattoos. The underwear selection that is clearly their own, not an item on a glossy US porn production budget. It feels quite an intimate scene, watching the solo boys, timing yourself to their timing, though I can't do the repeat shots (that final moment shown over and over, shot from a range of angles). One of them reminds me of a man I once fell for and remain fond of. A bittersweet viewing. ¶My home is a book-lined flat. In the living-room the books are arranged, wall to wall, in blocks of colour. There is space on the shelving for a television screen, under a row of huge eighteenth century books. It's where I might watch the videos. It's the room that my flatmates have often brought friends back to, handsome friends. Sometimes they've had sex in the room. Just the sight of a handsome man in this room, far more exciting to me than a man in my bedroom. When the boys, or their guests, pass through the living-room to the kitchen, they're often shirtless. Mostly unaware of the contents of the books that line the walls. Books there with the footnotes I've found fascinating, books and their omissions, where asterisks mark the spot. Bowdlerised books. All my older books, alongside the more recent hardbacks. Hardbacks – their dust-jackets taken off, naked, to let the sun or the lamp light catch their gold and silver stamped spines. My more academic collection is relegated to the hall, there's a section reserved for official "Gay Studies." ¶I've watched bodies in clubs for decades, I mostly prefer to stay home now. A certain weariness has set in. For all the adventures, I've finally tired of the gay scene, once my obsession. From gay liberation to government sanctioned forms of gay marriage. A withdrawal. I'm no longer anxious to pick up the weekly free gay papers, no longer keen to read the latest in gay studies, to see the newly opened gay film. I've stopped counting the gays on TV. I try to keep in touch with news from more dangerous states. I know that the work isn't over. I know I'm unlikely to stop writing, at least part of the time, on gay themes. I'm weary. *But the porn boys still arouse me.* ¶Porn plays its part in facing many things and in the avoidance of others. I'm never worried whilst watching it. When I'm with it, no mobile is allowed to ring, no e-mail can reach me. Nothing rushes through my mind, I forget the never-ending "to be done" list. Porn is curiously moving in relation to thoughts of age and death. The photo, the video, a record of something already over; though you watch it as if it is taking place, right now, just in front of and for you. Old porn might remind you of how the models must have aged, new porn reminds you of those who will. Memories of old lovers (or hoped for ones) is part of my porn viewing. Memories of some who are dead now.

If you look at it long enough...

But the memory is different to a more
ordinary memory. It eases and simplifies
past relations. It makes me more benevo-
lent, relieves me of responsibility,
sometimes of guilt. ¶Boys in video
boxes, by the books, including shelves of
rare and old erotica. All the reading, all
the searching, all the looking, all the
memories contained in the room. The
library would feel incomplete without
that screen. Of late I've been looking for
porn featuring books. Well, for naked
boys in rooms of books, naked boys
occasionally reading them. I've found a
few images. Should you happen to have
any, perhaps in your private collection,
let me know. Porn scenarios played out
against a backdrop of words. Flesh and
text. It's what I enjoyed with Pete and
his brother's drawer of porn. It's what I
enjoy now, forty years on. Porn tapes
and photos in the library. Live flesh in
the room is a bonus (and it does from
time to time happen). It's not essential,
or at least at this moment, it seems less
essential than it did. If that makes me a
sad old pervert, tucked away with my

porn, so be it. ¶Home Movie: My ideal would be a cum shot, the cum spilling onto the printed words, down the spines of the books. The spines naked with gold and silver lettering, the stains would remain and wouldn't wash out.

My own private pornography. A remnant, a reminder, like the cum-stained underwear on sale in many a gay magazine. A desire then for flesh against a backdrop of books, with minimal words, preferably foreign words, or broken English. Something not quite comprehended, certainly not there to be corrected. Like the words in Pete's brother's porn collection. Simple, limited, and to me at the time, oddly and pleasurably obscure. Men undressing and dressing in the living-room library. A couple of weeks ago there were two men in the living-room library. Guests of a flatmate, straight boys, one Greek, one French. They loved the room, they slept there on the pull-out couch. They were relaxed, comfortable, often shirtless. Sometimes just lounging, boxer shorts only. They flicked through the old volumes, noticed my bibliographies of banned books, the Victorian erotica, straight and gay. Picked up slang dictionaries, laughed at the language. The guests asked about the English for various words, for various acts. Neither appeared to have any problem with me, with my age, my sexuality. I think I detected a mild flirtation. Intensely erotic for me, the memory might become part of my porn repertoire. I lie, it already is. It's a memory now, I never take photographs. But for a diary note, I have no record. I don't keep a spycam, though it has crossed my mind. I enjoyed talking to them about London, showed them guidebooks to the city, old and new. Red-light districts included. I wouldn't have wanted to try anything, the moment was too perfect as it was. Besides, it would never have worked. Straight means straight sometimes, face it. Close, so close to my fantasy scenario. ¶The video surrounded by so many autobiographies, biographies, books of diaries; few of them even mention porn. There are diary-based details of every love affair, occasionally of every one-night stand. But few diarists consider a wank to a porn image worthy of atten-tion or mention. Samuel Pepys hinted at it once or twice, Gide too. Other diarists supply asterisks and codes. The great "Walter" of *My Secret Life* confessed all. Most of us take our memories of self-abuse with us to the grave. Many must be anxious to be rid of the source material before death. How many libraries, passed on, retain the owner's porn? I suspect my collection, fire or raid notwithstanding, will be with me till the end. I couldn't bear to see it go before I do. ¶Yes, porn is banal, repetitive, exploitive sometimes, but it isn't domestic; it is intense, but without the repercussions of desire. It's cleaner and less awkward than most encounters. It provokes a restless and insatiable need. Sometimes it substitutes for going out, for making an effort. It is a waste of time, but surely it's a glorious one. Surely, it makes us think in different ways about our pasts, our hopes. It allows an escape from the flesh and its imperfections; takes away some of the pain from ordinary relations; removes the aggravations and irritations of the day-to-day (unless, that is, the tape jams and to your fury unfurls in the machine). It might be a multi-million industry, but then again cheap copies are readily available. It's a well-known aid for insomniacs. I'd fallen asleep watching a porn tape on the night

Diana died. I woke to the news on TV. One of the first to know (useless knowledge). The tape had automatically switched off, and the BBC had returned. Some must have been watching old porn movies when Kennedy died or when Lennon was shot. No-one seems to give that answer to the "What were you doing on the day...?" question. Tasteless or not, it's also true I'd been watching a porn tape minutes before the live footage of 9/11 broke. I had just switched from video to the TV. I was the first to ring my friends, to tell them to turn on the TV. ¶Do I make too large a claim for porn, too many claims? Perhaps. I can only tell my own experience, and at some of the bleakest moments in my life, when all else seemed to fail, it obliterated, if only for half an hour, all thoughts of the deaths of family, the deaths of friends. More respected culture, working hard, and all those other tried and tested methods simply failed. They drew attention to the deaths, and perhaps brought useful tears. Porn just took the pain away. I feel a kinship with the

millions of others who wallow in porn,
find consolation in its confines. Porn

admits an absolute focus. But if it can
obliterate the thought of death, it also
has the sneaky habit of reminding you,

Paul Hallam

perhaps after the viewing, of the very thought it seemed to shut out. Orgasm has so often been described as "a little death," a poetic cliché. There are millions and millions of orgasms, forever spurting from the porn factories. ¶My porn fantasy home, featuring Paul Hallam (fully dressed) would be of a book-lined hotel-room. People passing through the hotel. Always changing, always fresh faces with a few older, retained favourites, remaining. From the window, passing bathers, palm trees and a view of the sea. The room supplied with all the latest in cable, satellite, digital. All the right switches. Waiters and repairmen would drop by. Boys might visit, spit and spoil, spunk all over my books, my room, my fantasy. Spurt all over my much abused self.

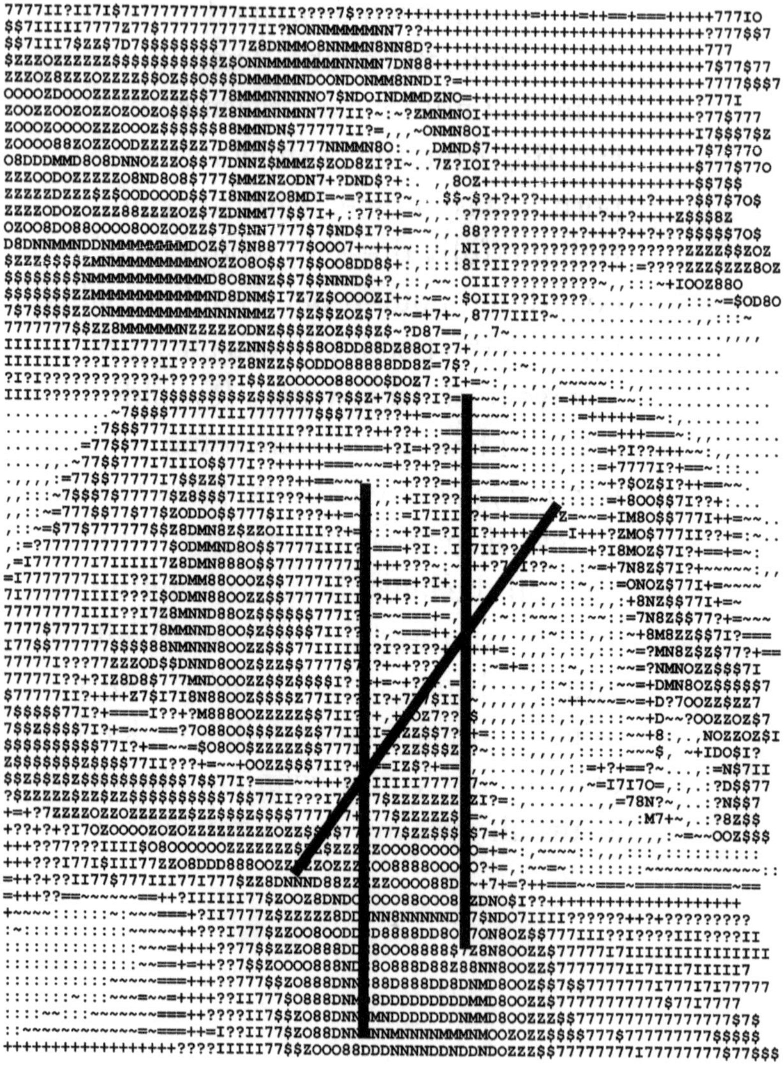

MONOGRAPHY

¶It is just over ten years since I wrote "If you look at it long enough..."; I realise I have had none of what some might call "proper," or even the more explicit, "full" sex since then. ¶Recently, a young friend asked whether I hoped to find a lover, a partner, someone my own age. Even I was surprised as to how quickly I said, "No." I had to think, why was I so definite? A second young friend asked, did I want, finally, to buy a place of my own. Again, a direct response, "No, even if I could." ¶"If you look at it long enough..." was published in 2004, in a special issue of the *Journal of Homosexuality, Eclectic Views on Gay Male Pornography: Pornucopia*, and simultaneously published in book form by Harrington Park Press. I was surprised that the editor, Todd G. Morrison, accepted and indeed welcomed the lengthy essay; it had, after all, only one footnote. It had none of the usual academic apparatus, and was entirely written in the much frowned upon first person singular, in an "I" voice. In it, "I" speculated on how the other, mostly academic contributors, might approach pornography. Would anyone mention their own "use" of it, or would everyone remain "detached"? ¶Looking at the writing again, I decided to leave it almost unchanged, that speculation included, for this new and very different "monograph" edition. The word "monograph" delights me, especially in relation to pornography. ¶The argument of the essay felt too interwoven to dismantle and re-edit it. It's an "involved" piece; even where a few phrases now strike me as awkward, I wouldn't want to interfere. I am playing with myself. ¶I found myself looking back over the ten years or so since its publication, and was surprised how much the essay had prefigured the future direction my erotic interests. ¶For much of the ten years before 2004, I lived in two of the then less salubrious areas of London. I rented a flat in Rupert Street in Soho for a while; much of it lit by the neon of the nearby venues, and then moved on to King's Cross. Rupert Street had a burgeoning gay scene at the time, and was still very much the territory of peep show parlours, pimps, drug dealers, strippers, prostitutes. I read that it had the highest crime rate of any street in Europe. To me, it was just my local area, nobody bothered me, we were all buying beer, cigarettes and snacks in the same shops at all hours. I kept an extensive notebook, what I saw and heard from my well-placed first floor window, fragments of conversations from the street. But when the BBC offered a large sum of money to film scenes for a costume drama in my flat, it became clear that the landlord wanted me to go. You didn't argue with Soho landlords. I moved with a new friend, met in Soho, to King's Cross, to an estate once described as "the worst estate in Britain." It had been "cleaned up," CCTV installed; someone was always on duty at the front desk reception. Over the years, and when the original friend moved out, I shared the three-bedroom flat with a number of new people who all subsequently became friends, all younger than me, all very sexual in a variety of ways. On the surface, it looked respectable enough, book-lined, with a teacher type responsible for the rent, and his young international lodgers. Being "good at words" I was able to help them with their English, often colloquial English. In 1995, I was a "writer in residence" at Central Saint Martins College of Art and Design, and also a part-time cultural studies tutor. My courses included Writing/Whoring, and Addiction in Art, and I was writing on pornography and prostitution at the time. But neither the landlord nor the neighbours needed to know the details of my writing or my teaching. My flatmates from the first, weren't really lodgers, it was not my own place; they were club scene sexual, ex-stripper sexual, escort sexual, porn video sexual; sometimes they were young men, "struggling" with mostly older ones, to pay their college fees. Some of the vice the estate had once been famous for

discreetly returned. King's Cross still had a gay porn cinema, a strippers' pub, seedy basements, and backrooms, it still had an atmosphere. Soho had been a solitary experience, from the window looking out. Now I had a warm and everyday shared experience, mostly shopping, meals, friendship, music and great conversations in and around the flat. Watching as the flatmates dressed and readied for the night, waiting up to see who they might return with. The atmosphere was almost always erotic, and the activities occasionally orgiastic. Many guests stayed overnight, or for longer, some stayed only for a paid for hour. Sometimes the flat became difficult, even lonely at times; people moved on, found partners, changed their ways. Finally I made the mistake of choosing a sweet but difficult flatmate, heavily into drugs and highly unreliable in paying the rent. I realised it was going to be impossible to keep the place on. ¶My pleasure in those years was mostly voyeuristic and vicarious. I had a few brief but memorable adventures of my own, but rarely felt I was lacking, or missing anything. There was all that was happening around me, and in my room, the Internet was filling with porn, chat-rooms were arriving, webcams introduced. Not that I always stayed indoors. I thought I had given up the gay scene, but I was encouraged out by the flatmate friends. A kind of last fling with the changing world of the pubs and clubs I had so often written about in the past. But it was wearing. In my fifties, I was finding London much harder than I thought, and my debts, accumulated over decades, were escalating. To move flat again, I would have to store a ton of papers and a massive library. ¶One evening, in 2004, setting out on foot to teach an evening class, I experienced what was later called a "neurological episode." I "lost" and yet remember the experience in detail, a few hours of my life in a hallucinatory state, a heaven and hell type experience, in the back streets of King's Cross. I didn't reach college. I remember trying to call to say I could not make it to the class, but I couldn't manage it. Somehow, I did eventually find the way back to the flat. I knew I was close to home when the handsome Turkish man from the local kebab shop saw me passing and rushed out to ask if I was alright. It was clear to him I was not. I had no idea what the time was, or what I was supposed to be doing, and I didn't think to get to a hospital. The next day, my local doctor was astonished that I had not immediately rushed to the nearest hospital Accident and Emergency department. ¶Hospital appointments were quickly booked, mostly at the National Hospital for Neurology and Neuroscience, but at other major hospitals, and at more local clinics too. A great range of tests were conducted; I was subject to all manner of scans. For once I was being looked at, with thoroughness, care and immense skill; I was watching myself, and all the versions of me, the medical world could offer. I felt strangely calm and peaceful under the MRI scan. And I had never been asked so many questions about my "history." ¶A brief medical history unreliably related: I was born at home, in Garden Road, Mansfield, and then rushed to hospital. Mum was told that I would probably not last the night. A rapid christening was arranged. ¶All I was ever told was that my mum took my blood. But I survived. ¶As a child, I was quite fit and more or less "normal"; very bright at speaking, reading and writing; useless at just about everything else. But from time to time I dropped down in the street, or in school, or on any floor, and my body went completely rigid. So much so that people who saw me assumed I was dead. But slowly I would come round. ¶The local doctor told my Mum that I would "grow out of it" and she was not to worry. I did grow out of it. ¶In 2004, I carried on teaching, and went for an extensive memory test at the National Hospital for Neurology and Neuroscience. They found me fascinating. I had the highest score in the "word" test they had ever seen (100/100, an unheard of result), and one of the lowest scores on logic and mathematics. Unbelievable for someone at my

level of education, they said. Almost
zero. I was shown some old photographs
of men with highly distinctive 1970s
haircuts. A visual memory and recogni-
tion test, I think. The photographs were
the same ones used when the test was

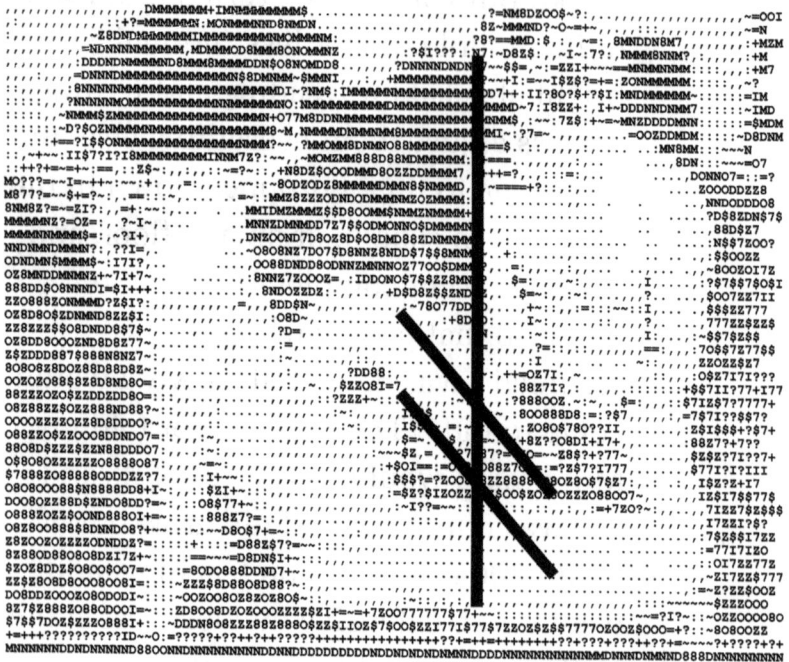

invented, they explained. I was very
good on remembering haircuts of the
Seventies. ¶What I didn't know was that
they were observing and assessing my
panic levels throughout the procedures.
I mostly achieved very high levels of

panic. ¶Depression, drink and debts were discussed, and I followed up on suggestions and advice, but I insisted I was not suicidal; and no-one seemed to think there was much connection with any of that to the "episode" anyway. They were hugely helpful and wrote letters to support my appeal for a one-bed local authority home. Even so, all my appeals failed. I was well enough to work, I was a single man, and they wouldn't even put me on a waiting list. There were times when I was pretty close to the street, embarrassed and exhausted by having to ask yet another friend for a spare couch. ¶In the end, apart from some minor nerve disorder, and they really looked at me in every medical/psychological way possible, they just had to declare, to my guarded relief, that I had experienced a "neuro-logical episode." But they did add that this might be a return of what they thought was probably my childhood epilepsy. ¶Not long after months of consultations, conversations, tests and scans, I was invited to show *The Last*

Biscuit, a collaboration with Andrea Luka Zimmerman, part a film portrait of me, part autobiography, at a conference at Haliç University in Istanbul, on "Life Writing." I had never been to Turkey before, I jumped at the chance. I arrived on the eve of my 54th birthday, in April 2006. The arrival started badly with the loss of my guidebook; I had copied the university contact list, the hotel name, notes on transport and a few Turkish phrases into the back of it. I was totally lost. By midnight, after a generous taxi driver rescue, and much wide-eyed wandering, I toasted my birthday; more significantly, I resolved that I would one day live in Istanbul. After the week-long visit, it was only meant to be for three days, I announced the decision to my closest friends back in London. The idea met with some incredulity. ¶I could only say it was love, love at first sight, I was in love with a city. My friends must have winced at the gush; I was oblivious to both criticism and practical considerations at the time. It was not just the sight of the city itself. I had met a group of friends through a literature student at the conference; he invited me to stay for longer in Istanbul, if I didn't mind a couch in a typical student flat. He introduced me to many of his closest friends, not all of them students. And those friends introduced me to their friends, and to their versions of the city. A group of straight young men: more into heavy metal bars than famous mosques. Within days, they appeared to have adopted me, though some later came to call me "uncle," or "older brother," or even a "second father." Protective words perhaps, let's make everything familial. I was invited to stay longer, or at least to come back as soon as possible. There would always be places to stay with them. Longer and longer visits followed, sometimes lasting several months. Two years later, I was fully a resident. ¶In London, my friends have always been incredibly mixed, all sexualities, all gender variations. I realised, within a few visits, that in Istanbul I was in a different world to my usual one. I have only a fleeting relation to gay politics/culture here, and I had decided I really was too old for the late-night club scene. Before Soho, I had my share of one-nighters, short and more serious longer-term relationships. But from the mid-nineties, I had lost any hope for, or perhaps even interest in, long-term partnerships, and had zero personal interest in the idea of "gay marriage" except as an "equality issue," but one that still seemed to leave, on so many levels, singles unequal. ¶In London, the best times were often on the side-lines of wilder lives than mine. My experience in Turkey, has felt, still feels, very different. I've found an easy and mostly relaxed friendship with straight men. Some of the younger ones had little or no sexual experience at all. Several had never knowingly met a gay man before; I had a lot of explaining to do. Others were surprisingly open about their own sexual encounters, frustrations, and the business of not, for various reasons, finding it easy to find "full" or "proper" sex. I smiled benignly. I met with no hostility, and only once with some suspicion and fear. He brought a friend along when we arranged to meet at a teahouse. When, on a later occasion, he came alone, he carried a knife. He only told me that months later. He was to become one of my greatest friends. Being quickly "out" with new friends in Turkey has not always been easy. The good friends introduced me to other friends, and often their families, with no mention of my being gay. Why would I tell them that, they asked. That's personal, that's private. Because it would save me having to do it at some point, at least with your friends, was my reply. ¶The first connections, with many friends here, were much to do with their curiosity about England and America, and a major desire to improve their English. I have been a conversational English teacher in Istanbul, though I have stopped all teaching now. Inside of college I felt somewhat constricted, the first and only native English speaker at the Foreign Languages Department at Istanbul University in my first year of working there. Responsibility enough, with hundreds of students, I was too nervous to also "come out," even though a good deal of my early writing had concerned the importance of just that. I was not even "out" as a writer at the university. But a few students searched my name on the Internet, and privately and quietly let me know they liked the sound of my work. They appreciated it. ¶I was very struck by one friend's remark; he said he talked to me about things he would not talk about in Turkish. This could be about politics, about family horrors, more often it was about sex. Listening to their stories, or reading them on various forms of Messenger. Watching less pornography, but imagining their adventures related to me instead. My relationship to porn was changing perhaps. I have been hugely attracted to three friends in almost ten years of being here. But I can only write about them through highly disguised fiction, which I am at work on now: a book and a film. It is too close to home. Too close in time, in one case, still raw, and all three remain great

Paul Hallam

```
80008DDDD8OZ8DDD800088888888DD8888088DDD8DD8O88OZZ08OOZZ$$$Z$$Z$ZZZ7$ZOZ$Z$$+OOZ
DDOZZZZ8D8ZZZ$$OZ$Z$7$$$$$OO888O8O8ZZZZZZZ$$$$$$$$77$ZZ77ZZZOZ77Z$OOZZZ8ZZ7$.Z
OZOOOZOOOZOOZOD8888OO8O8DDDD8OZ7ZZZZZZZZZ77$ZO88OZOOZ77$ZOZ$77$ZOOOOZZZ$O8Z,OO
DDDD88O88O8OOZ$ZOZOO88OOO8O$$$$MMNO???I+M88ZZZZ$$7IIIII77?I77II77$7$Z$OOO8D
$77$$7$$$$7$$$$$ZO88OZZ$Z$ZNNZ$M+N7MMM:OD$$$ZZ$Z$$$OOZZOZ$$OOZ$$77$ZZZO$ZOZ
ZOOZZ$ZZ88DNNNNNNNNNNNNDDD8NM8MDMMM    MZMN7NMOD8DDDOOZZZOZZ808O88OOOZZ$ZOOZZO.$ZZ
MNNNNNNNMNNNDDD888DDDDNNND8OMM:MMNMM   ZZMI=MMMZ$$$OZOOO$$$$Z$ZZ$$$$ZOZZ$I$$$$?
NNNNNNNNNDD888OOZZ$$Z$$OZ$MMOD7MMMM   M8MMMMNM$ZOOO88O7ZZ$7I$$$$OZ$$77$$$77$$ZZ
NNNDDNDD8DDD888OZZ$$77$$$MM8ZNMMMMM   77DZ?MMM8ZODDDD8D8O8O88OO8ZOOO8ZZ$ZOZ7$ZZ
800088D88OZZOO88DD8888DD8M+:8MMMMDN   NM7NNMMMM888O8Z$Z$$ZZ$OO$ZZO$OZZOZZOOZ7.$7Z
OO88D888DNNNDD888D8D8D8?Z:MODMM+NN   +MZ?MMMMNO8D8888DD8ZZ$ZODDDDDDDDDDDDDD8DDZ
8OZZOOZZOO$OO8ODDDD888OOZ~,?MNMOINM   MM~NMDID7O88OD8D88D8DD8888OO$088OZZZ$OZZ
ZZZO888OZZO888ZZZZ$888D~?=7~8I8MMM   MMMNMM888NNNNNDDDNDDDNNNNNDDDZZOD888Z8D,OZ
$ZZ88ZZZ$ZO88NNNNNNNNN?==~::7IIONMD  NDNDMMZ$:OO8$OOOOZOO8O8O8D888DDDDDNNNNNNNZ
7$$ZOODD8DDNNNDDDNNDN7I?+==$77:O8Z  8DD8$7$+:.ODZOOZZOOZOZ888D88888DDDDDD7$.DZ
ZZZZ$$$O8DDDD8888888$77I   ++=II?77D 8D8Z$IO?=:..77$$ZZOZZOOZOZZO8OZOOOZ7.OZZ
$7$$Z$$$$$$ZZZZOOZ$$7$$$7I  $NIZ8N8 O8888$Z7?~,...,7$$ZOOO$$O88O$$$O$$7$OOO8ZO
DDDD8OZZZZOO88DZ$$+=??I$OZID  NZ88D Z8O8D88Z?~:,.....$$Z$$$OOOO888OZ$$$ZOOZZ8OZ
8DOD8OO888D8O8DND+~~==+$NNNMMM  O8D 8OO8DD8$+~:,.....,+$ZOOZ8O8D88O$$$7ZZ$$ZZDZ
DDDO8Z88OZ88OZ$Z+=~~=+?7MNNMMMMM  DDDNNNN~,,.........$ZO8OZZZZ7OO8O88DDZ
D8D888DDD8DDND0?+++=?I7DMDNMMMMMMM NNNMN8?,,,,......~Z7$7$ZZOODDZODZ$ZODZ
ZO8OOOZZOO$7$7++~=ZO8DNMMDNMMMMMMMM MMD?Z7I+:,,:~:,,.,:ZDD$OO8DDDNNNNNNNNND
$$ZOO8D8ZZ$$7+~::~7NNMNONMMMMMMMM  MMM 7I+++++=~~=+~:,,,:NDNDNDDNNODDDDNNNNDZ
ZOZO8O$$$ZO8$?==$DDO8OO88DOZZZOOZO  MNN8 I?+++=~~=+~:,,:,?ND8D8DDD8DDDD8D8DDZ
$7ZOZOZOO8$Z777IOZ$ZZOZOO8O$$ON7+  +?++  +===+?II+~:::~~$$$$Z$Z88DDDD88Z
Z$$OOOZZZ$ZO$77$7$7771$$ZO8O:...,=:  ~,:=++++=~~==I+~:~Z$$7OZZ$Z8$$Z8ZZOZ
OOOO8O88ZZO??????77IIIO7$ZI+~,.~:+?I  +Z7+++++I???I888I=:,,=8O88$7$$ZOO8OZZZOZ
O8Z8DNDD8D8D+=~+?II8ZZ7$?7~,O,,O?, II?7?+???I$O8DNMO+~:,,,,:Z$7$OZ$OZ88OZO8OZ
D8888ODD8DDDD8DDNDD8OOZ77+$~:7~.~~, +==~$7III7$OONMMMZ7?~,,,,7ZZZZ$$OZZ$$$ZZ
NNDDDDOOZOOD8O$OZOO8I7?7I:M7=.?~   ,,::~:,:::,OMMDIDO?~,,.,$8888OOOZ$$$ZO7OO
NDD8888D888DDDOZO8DODN8,8:D$,MN+, ::~,,::,,,,,,,88Z+~,,:$Z8ZZDNNNNNDDDZZZ
$$$8D8DNNDDDNNNDDZ$$8D87~~7+N=,DD7: +~~~=~,::,,,,,,O$=:,,:NDDDDDDDNNDDOZ
DNNN88OZO8888D8DDDODZO88+.IINO~D7+=M I+==~7+~,,::,,,I?=:::~D88O888OD88DO
NN88DNNNNNNN8Z88O888D:OZ=+,D,7$77 III$$7I=~:~=~~~:,,,,Z+=~::~D7ZO888D88888OOZ
................  ..088I77O$77$ ?77Z8DZI????I??=~:,,,+=:,:~NDNDDD8D8DDDZ
...                .088DII78DO7 7I7$NM$OZZ$$OOZ$?+~:,,,,~:::$888888DDNNZ
...              .8888D775$MMM 7$$$ZZOOZ7IO88OOZ7?=~,,,,:,::DNNDNDDOZOOOO
.........==+==~,....DODDNN7IIDMM OZODND8OOZZ$II888O8ZI+~:,,,,,+O$8NNNNMNN
.....:++++++NMMMDM=+?+7DMOO8DN7NMMM~ $Z8DDDNMMNDO$ZZ$OOZOO7?=~~=~:,,,,MDD8DDDDD8D
.....+++??$.+MMNI??OOND8OO8OINMMMM $OODD8DDDDDDNOOO8807+~,=+~,,,,?DDDDNNND
........$7$$$$$$$I777DD88D8NNN77NMMMM=8NNDDD88888DD8NNNOO8O7~,,+~:,,,,?DNNNNNN
........I?I?77$$$ODNDD888MMMI1MM7ZM MNNNDDDD8888888DDNNMMMNOOI=7+:,,,,,,DNN
,......??II$$ZZDDNNND87$I:I+,D+M.? ,NMMNDDDDD888888DDNNMMMNOOI=7+:,,,,,.INDZ
......O8DDNNNMDNNND8788?DNMZ$M+MMD =,I7NDDDOO77777$DODDNNMMMM888Z7O7=:,,,,.INDZ
.....,,$8DDNNDNNNDD8Z7D.OM?MOO~?$O :I?+$NDDD8O7II??+==:~,.ZNMMN8O8Z8O?:,,,,
......:IDDNNOODNDNDDND8$ZM?Z7$II=++ =?$O7MNNDDDOZZ$$7I+=:,....,NMMDD8O8ZO+:,,,,
....:~?DM~==~7NNDD8NINMMM8$+~=I=~, ,,,ZMMNNDDDD8?:,,....,DDD8N,O8ZD$=:,
...:~+M~~:::,D:=D8DDMMMMD$++=:,~ ,,,,MMMNNNNDII7~:,,.....D8Z,.NMOO8Z+:,
..~=~=~:~:::D,~:N7ZMMMM8Z7?=:, ,~:?MMMMNNZOOZ~:,,,.....8$=,NNNMN88?:
...~~=~~~::::~~~:D~OMMMNN  I8ND=,7MMMMN8ZDD~,,,,,,,,,.....$+.,DDNNMNO
....+=~~~~~:::::~~~=8Z8,~8?, DI,.:,+,+MMMMNON?:,,,,,,,,.....=...8DNDNO
.....~=~~~~~:~::~~~~==M=,D=ID+=  D,.:~~=:MMMMMNZ:,,,,,,,,,......7.....:D
.....~~~=~~~~:~~~~~~~~+IM,.,$,DI=I+ D,,,,~~=$$7MMMMMN:,,,,,,,,......O..
.:~~~~~~:~~=++?I7OM$7,~:77I+? ~:,,~:+MMMMM?:,,,,,,,,,......$.......
...~~:~~~:::::~+I7$Z8MMM8$$$8I$7I?+ +2+,MMMM?~:,,,,,,,.,,:O=?7I77I
=~~~~~~~:::~~+I$ZDDMMMIDOO8OZO$I+ 8Z77~,$MZ:,,,,,,,,,:,,,DMD$7II7I7
$$$Z~~~~~~~~~+?Z88O.:M88NN=+DO8D$ ,+=DDD?~7=:,,,,,,,,,,:~DMNO7I?I
7Z$ZZO$$OO77Z8D,,,,,D~:,,,+=?ND8O$ +?~NMNDI:,,,,,,,,,,,,:=ZMMNMI?,.
$ZZ$OZ$OZ7Z77OO::,::,,,,,,=~=NNNM DNI:MMM8+~:,,,,,,,,,,,:~+,MNM88M++
$$ZZZZOZOZZOZZOZ~~::,,,,,,:,==7$NNM MMMMMM7=~:,,,,,,,,,::::~=~:+~MMMD88
ZOOOOOOOOO7ZZO~::,,,,,,,:,:=7$NNM=M MMMMMM7+=~:,,,,,,,,,:~~=I+IMMMNN88
8Z8OOOOOOOOOZ=~:,,,,,,::,,~=I$MMMM MMMMM7+=~:,,,,,,,::~~~~=+??7NMMMMNN
..:~:+$8OZZ$O$=~=~~:,,,:::,:=7MMM=M MMMMM?==:~:,,,,,,:~~=++??II78MMMMMNNNNN
...    .=~~~~~:,,,,:~,+=MMM:NNMMM8+=~:,,,,,,::::=+?I7O88DMMMMMMMMMMN
...   .=====~~=~:,,,,:~:~MMM~NMMMMI?~::::::,::::~=+?IZNMMMMMMMMMMMMMN
.......,+=++++=+===~:::~=IMMM7MMMMI7~::::::~:~~=?7OONMMMMMMMMMMMMM
...I,:,~=+=~=?+?I?++=~=~~=?IMMMOMMMM$?==~:::~::~=~==?INMMMMMM.....=+=+$...Z
..,.:,~~++++??+??I?+++++=~=+N8ZMMMMMD7?==~:~:~~~=~+INMMMM.=~~~=~:~::~N..
=+,~=++?+??+++DN8$7IIIIII??I~ZNDMMMMMMD7?==+=~::~=~+IMMMM.:+=~~~~:::N..
,.~=+????+?+?+DNZ7I77I77?I+:~MMMMMMMMMO7?==~~:~:~~=+I$MMM,:+=~~~~::::,M...
?===+????????+NNZZ$II7777+=~~MMMMMMMMMZ7?+=~=~~~~~=+?7DMM.~+=~~~~~:,,~,$...Z
===+++?????TT7NNNN8O$$T??+=== MMMMMMMMMOZT?+=~~=~~~++?TMM..?+~=:~...
```

friends. ¶Pornography for me these days is more a kind of "supplement" to experience. So much of pornography seems to be about completion, leading to the final shot. So many relationships seem incomplete, sometimes unlikely, others impossible. And afterwards remembering how far the acts went, often with pleasure. But perhaps more often, the destination not reached, or the offer or opportunity missed, or if taken, botched. The wrong move. You got so far, but no further. Rejection. A move towards a completion, not necessarily of something "full," but of the act you most hoped for. Too embarrassed to ask for something, or if you did ask, you were perhaps denied it. Brief moments and awkward encounters can be added to with a porn video. But more often than not now, I rapidly lose interest in the video. ¶I think my pornographic taste now is more old-fashioned. Conversation or even telephone sex, but with people I know, not on "chatlines," as they were once called, or in pay-per-minute one-to-ones with models in "private" rooms on porn sites. I think it concerns words more, a language exchange. I was very good at words, they told me at the hospital. I enjoy the sound of Turkish, a language I still don't understand or speak; it gives me relief from hearing the "everyday" conversations around me. I love the often haltering conversations in English I experience every day though. Not knowing Turkish offers a welcome solitude at times. It's not all words of course, there are still the visuals; I have moved flats five times since moving to Istanbul. Five rooms, five different areas, different atmospheres and views from the windows. Repeated walks and watching from windows. Each room, with its own distinct erotic. Shared places or solitary, with furniture and with histories not my own. I live lightly now, with a view to reducing my own possessions to two trunks, perhaps even two suitcases. I go out much less than I used to. I try to avoid as many invitations as I can to exhibition openings, film previews, weddings, indeed any family event, to

group occasions at which, understanda-
bly and inevitably, even polite, English
speaking, Turkish friends speak in
English for a while, then slowly slip
back into Turkish. ¶The less than full or

```
▓▓▓▓~~~~~~~I78$III?????III+?$ZZ$7777$$OD+═══+═══════════+═══~+══~═+══~═+══~═~══════+7?═══════++++═I$ZZZZZZZZO8
▓▓▓▓~~═~IOZ77II?III??+?78O$$78$$ZOO8═══════+═══+═══+═══~~═+════?══════+I7?═+═+═══+++═I$ZZZZZZZO
▓▓▓▓~═~═~══?O$$7IIII7????I$$Z$$$$ZO8DI═══+═══════+═══+═══+═══════════II+++++++++I$OZZZZZZZO
▓▓▓▓═~═~══DZ$777II?78$7$OO$$ZZO88N+═══+═══════+═══+═══════════II+++++++++I$OZZZZZZZO
▓▓~══+++═~~~~7OO$77?7?+7$OO8DO77ZO88DO+++═++++═+══+++++═══+══II++++++++?ONZZZZZZOO
▓▓~~~~═══~~~~~~OZZ7I7$78$$ZOZDO$ZZ88DD?+═+═══+++++++═══+++++═══+══?I7+++++++?8DZ8ZOZOOO
▓▓═══~═══~~~IO$78Z7I$Z$78$ZO88DD7++++++═+═══++═══+═══+══+════?I7++++++++?7ZZZOZOOOO
▓▓═══~═══~═~+7$$Z$$OO888 B8D888NI++?+++++++═+++++++++++═══+══II+++++++++?$ZZOOO
▓▓═══~~═~═~~~═+$$ZZZZZZZO B888DD7++?????++++??7+++++++++++═══+7+═══?II?++++++++7ZZZOOO8
▓▓═══~══~══$Z8OZZO888 BDDNDD8++???++++++?+++++++++++?II?++++++++7ZZZOOOO8
▓▓═════~═~══════$ZO8OOZO8D DDNNDDD8O$I??+7++++?++++?+══+++═+++?II++++++++7ZOZOZOOO8
▓▓═══~══~══~I$ZZZDDNNDD NNNNDDDDNNN??????+?+++??+++++++++7III++++++++I ZOZOOO
▓▓═══~═════DZ$$ZOO+?7$$ DD8$DNNNNNNNNM+?????++?+??+7++++═+++?++++++?II7+++++++++I$OZZOOOOO
▓▓══════=?NDDNN$$Z$+,═:~~~~~IMNNNNNNNNN$????+????????+++++++++?++++?II7++++++++?$OZZOOO
══════ZN8ODMMDDDDNNNND8Z??═+++++7+═M?ONNNNNNNNNNNNN$I??????+??+++?++++++7++++++II7++++++????$OZZO
???INNDDDDDDDDNNNNNND$??I7I77 IIII77ONNNNNNNNNNNNNNNN???+????+?+++++?7++++III++++++????$OZOOOOOO
???DDDNNDDDDDNNNNNNNN$????7771?I IIII77ONNNNNNNNNNNNNNNZIIII??????++???????++?III++++++??+$OOOOOOOO
??7DDDNNNDDDNNNNNNNNN7I?+?IIII77 7IIIIIZNNNNNNNNNNNNNNNOII??II?????????+?+??+?7++++III+++++??+7OOOOOOO
??8DNNNNDDNNNNNNNNNNN7771?IIII7 87II7IZNNNNNNNNNNNNNNN7I???III7I??????+??7+++?II7++++?+?7OZOOOO
??MDNNNDDNNNNNNNNNNNM77771?III7I IIIIIIZNNNNNNNNNNNNNM????I7I$ZI?????+?I????+?II7++++?+?7OOOOO
?7DNDDDNNNNNNNNNNNNN777771IIIII IIII+I?+7MDNNNNNNNND8?IIIII77$ZO?????+??????+??7II?++++++IZOOOOOO8
?IDNNDNNNNNNNNNNNMDN777771I??7I IIII++═══+═DNNNNNNNN$IIII777$$ZO7??????7I???+++?I?7++++IZOZOOOOOO8
?IDDDNDNNNNNNNNNN$NN7I══════?I7 7771771?++7++8NNNNNM7IIIII7$$$ZOZ?????+?????++?II++++??+?ZOOOOOO8
?7NNNDDNNNNMNNNNNNNN$III??══ ══+7ZZ7?I$778DNNNNNM87IIII77$$ZO8?I??????+?+++?II++++?????8ZZOOOOO
?7DNNDDNNNNDNNNNNNNMZ$7771?I??+? II$$I$$ZO8?7NNNNNZ7IIII777$$ZOO7??+?I???+?+++?II7++++????8ZZOOOO0
?7$NNDDDNNN8O8NNNNMZ$7771I$8OOZ $$$777$OZ8DDDZDNNNNZ$7III177?I$ZOO7??+?7????+?++?III+++++????ZO8ZOOO
?IONNNNNNOD8DNNNNNZ$771I?I?7+? $ZZOZZZOOOO8DO$$NNNNZ$771II77$$ZO8?7II??????+?+??I?I+++++?+?8OZOOO
?I$NDDOOOO8NMNMND$$$7IIII771?+ $ II?77$$$ZZ88OO$$MDOO$77777$$$ZOO8??++?????+?I7II7++++??+?8OZOOOO8
??7OD8NNNNNNNO7777III7$Z$I77$ 7ZZ$$$$7$$$$O8OO$$888Z$777$$ZZOON?+?????+═?7I7II++++?+?7$OZOOO08
?I7ZNMNNNDNNNZ$7777777$ZONIIII $ZZZZZZ$Z$$O8OZZZ$ZD8$77777$$ZZO88?+++??++══+I?7II?+++++??$OZOOO
?I7$NN8NNNM$7777777$ZZZOD$I?77 ZOOO88OZ$$SZO88ZZOOZO$7II77$$ZO8N+++?7??+++++═I7I?++++++??7OOOOOOO88
?IIZ88NNNZ777I77$$Z$Z8ZI???I7 $ZZZZ$7I$O8OOZZZZOOOZ7II77$$ZO88O++?+?+?═+═?7IIII?+++++7OOOOOO088
?I78DNND777777777I$$$ZZ8OI????7 $87$ZZ$ZO8OOZ$$$$$$$$7II7$$ZO8DI++++═??77I++══?77II?++++?+?OOOOOO
?I7DNNO7777777I$$$ZZ8OI?????7 ZOZOOODDZZOO8OOOO8$ZZO8$777$$ZO8N?+++═+I?+═+++?7II?++++I?I0000000
?II788777I77777$$$$OOO7II?I7?+? 8OOOOOODNMMMNZOOOOOOO8DDD8877$$ZOO8?7??++++++?7+═?7III7+?+?77IZ8OOOOO08
I778777777777I77$$$ZO8D$7IIIII77$ $$$ZZZZO0MMMMMMZZOO88DD8D7$$$ZOO8Z═??+++++++??+═?7?III?+?+?????$8O00
77777777777$$$$ZZ8DO7IIIII77 7I7$$ZZZZZOONNMMMM0800888888D$$$$ZZO88I++++++++?7+═?7III?++?+??7$8OOO
7777777777$$$$$ZOODZ$IIIIIII7I 77$$ZZZZOODMMMMMOOOOO888880DO$$$ZO88+++═══+═+?7I?I++═?7IIII?7?+????$8OOOOOO08
77777$$$$ZZZOO8D$7IIII?7IIII7? 777$$ZOOO8NMMMMMZZOOOO88D8D$IIIII7?═══+═══+?+?7I?I?++?7III?7?+?$OOOOO
778$$$$ZZZZOO8DO7????????7I77 777$ZZOOO8NMMMMMMZZ88888800O8ZZZZOZZZ$$I7II?????????7I77D8D8
$$$$$$ZZZZOODD8ZI?????????IIII? 777$ZZOOO8NDNMMMMZZOO8088008DOZZZ$$$ZZZZZZ$$$$SII?????????+?Z8O8NNDOO
$$$$ZZZ2000D8DO$7??????7IIIIII 77$$ZZOO88DNDMMMNZO$OOOO88O88888888888O7777777?7$$$$$SIII??????????7IO000
$ZZ2ZOOOOD8O2$7I??????7IIIIIII 77$$ZZOO88DNNN$7$OOO88888888888DOIIIII77777777IIII?????????7780000000
ZZZO888780O2$$7771I?????IIIIII 77$$ZO088DN77I$$$ZOO888888888888IIIIII7777III7IIIII??????????78D0000
O00O8OI??I00$77771II??????I7I7 $$ZOO088D07I7$$ZOO888888888DD8D77IIIIIIIIIIIIIII??????????ODOOOOOO
O08OO????O2$77771IIIII???I77 7$$ZOO888D$$IIIZE$$OOOO08888888DD8D8??IIIIIIIIIIIIIIIII??????????780OOOO
88??????????IZ$78$$7771IIIIIIII77 7$ZOO888BD8$77$$77ZOO888888DDDDD???7III?IIIIIIIIIIIIIII??????????780000
$?????????????78$$771I7771II77777 7$ZOO088D80$8$$7770888888888DDDDN7????7IIIIIIIIIIIIIIIIII??????????7800
+????????????78$$7771I7777771III $$ZZOO088D$$77770888888888DDDDO?????????7IIIIIIIIIIIIIIIIIII??????780O8O
+???????????$$$$$7777777771IIIIII 77$$ZZOO88Z77I7088888888DDD$????????7IIIIIIIIIIIIIIIIIIII????780080
???????????????7ZZ$$$7771IIIIIIIII 77777777$OO8D$77777II8888888DDN??????I?????7IIIIIIIIIIIIII?????788
????????????IZ$$$77777777771I I77777?$$ZO8$7777I7D8888DDDDI??I?I????7IIIIIIIIIIIIIII??????70800008
????????????ZZ$$7777777771I$ IIII7777$ZO8$7777770807771D888887III?IIII????7IIIIIIIIIIIIII??????7Z80O0
????????????ZZZZ$7I7771I7777 IIIII777$ZO88877$$77II7I7II7III??IIII?I????IIIIIIIIIII???????7$80000
??????????????Z$$Z$7777777771$ IIIII777$ZOON8$??77777777777IIII?I?I?I????IIIIIIIIIII?????7I$
????????????7Z$$Z$7777771 7IIIIIII77$ZZOO8O??7777$7$7777IIII?I??I?I?I????IIIIIIIIIIII????7I780
???????????????I$$Z$$$7$7$$7? 7IIIIIII7$$ZZOO888O7777$$$$8DOO8$IIIIIIIIIIIIIIIIIIIII??I??I?I780008
I??????????????IOZZZ$$$$$$$$$7 7IIIII77777$$ZZOO88877$$NDNDDNDDDDDDMIIIIIIIIIIIIIIIIIII??IIIO800
?I????IIII????????7ZOOZZZ$$$$$ 777I7777777II77$$$ZZZOO77$$NDD88DDDDDM=7IIIIIIIIIIIIIIIIIIIIII??IIIIZ80808
II???????I?????????ZOOZZZ$$$$$ $77777771I77$$$$$$ZZOO7$DNNNNNNNNDOZNZIIIIIIIIIIIIIIIIIIIIII
??????????I?????I?IIZOOZZZZZ$$ $$$$$$8?II7777$$777D88888DOOOO0OOOO00IIIIIIIIIIIIIIIIIIIIIII$DOO
??II?II???II?IIIIIIII$OOOZOZZ Z$Z$$7IIIIIIII7IIII7$$ZZOZ$O8888888880$IIIIIIIIIIIIIIIIIIIII7D0008
?IIIIIIII?IIIIIIIIIIIZOOOZOZ ZZ$$$7?I????IIIIIIIIII778$ZZON&MSZOZ$$$$$$$IIIIIIIIIIIIIIIIIIII7D0008
?IIIIIIIIII?IIIIIIII$ZOOZ$$$ $$$$$7?????IIIIII77$$ZZOON$$$$$$7777IIIIIIIIIIIIIIIIIIIIII7
?IIIIIIIIIIII?IIIIIIZ$ZOOZZ$ $$$$$I?????7IIIII??77$$ZZOON8ZZZZZ$$777IIIIIIIIIIIIIIIIIIII88O
?IIIIIIIIII??IIIIIIIIZ$8OOZ$$77I???7IIII7?IIIIII77$$ZOOOZ$$$$$$$7777IIIIIIIIIIIIIIIIIIIIO0O88
?IIIII??????I?IIIIIIII$ZON8OZ$7771?????IIIIIII7$$ZZOOOO8$$$S$$7777IIIIIIIIIIIIIIIIIIIIIIEDO
????IIIIIII?IIIIIIIIII$Z8NDD88Z$771IIIIIIII17$ZZOOO8OO$$77771IIIIIIIIIIIIIIIIIIIIIIIIIIIIIII
IIIIIIII?IIIIIIIIIIIIIIZZZ$NDDO$$7771IIIII7I7I7777$ZOOOO88$777I7III7IIIIIIIIIIIIIIIIIIIIIII7$DO8
IIIIIIIIIIIIIIIIIIIIIIIZZ8NNDDZ$7777777777777777$$$ZOOOO08$$$7771I7$77IIIIIIIIIIIIIIIIIIIIIIII7$8OO
```

proper sex has amounted to little more than a furtive glimpse, an occasional feel, not initiated by me, I hasten to add. Only in a hamam, or by the sea do most men readily take their shirts off. My most recent move has been to an island. I snatch copies of photographs off Facebook of friends I love looking at, and marvel at how new technology allows me to be able to use close-up and crop. I admit, the friends are rarely my "own age." Even when I was much younger I liked men in their mid-late twenties, often at some kind of turning point in their life, wilder days often ending. ¶Sometimes I will be watching pornography, but looking at a photograph, or out of the window, or simply remembering the rare sexual contact, and usually, the real life takes over, or intermingles with a few minutes of porn. The rooms, even family homes I've visited, might become part of it. ¶I imagine people I know in their homes or hometowns, in the places I've visited with them, or places they tell me about, where they've been with a new girl.

¶Much of "If You Look" is still how I think about pornography. But other thoughts have emerged, and perhaps that is very much to do with age. In fantasy I have no sense of my own aging body. It's strange: I am in on the act, and yet I never picture me. If I do make a rare appearance, I am always clothed. I prefer to keep some cover, even on my own, even in fantasy. There are more fragments of dialogue in my recent fantasies, conversations remembered. Sometimes the fantasies leave me happy, sometimes not. Whatever, I make do. In the "real" world I doubt I would want to go "all the way," even were the chances to be offered. Perhaps the fantasies have taken over now, and maybe they are not just making do, after all. Perhaps I take more pleasure in the new settings, in a fuller range of senses, in the elaborate detour.

Paul Hallam
October, 2015
Istanbul, Turkey

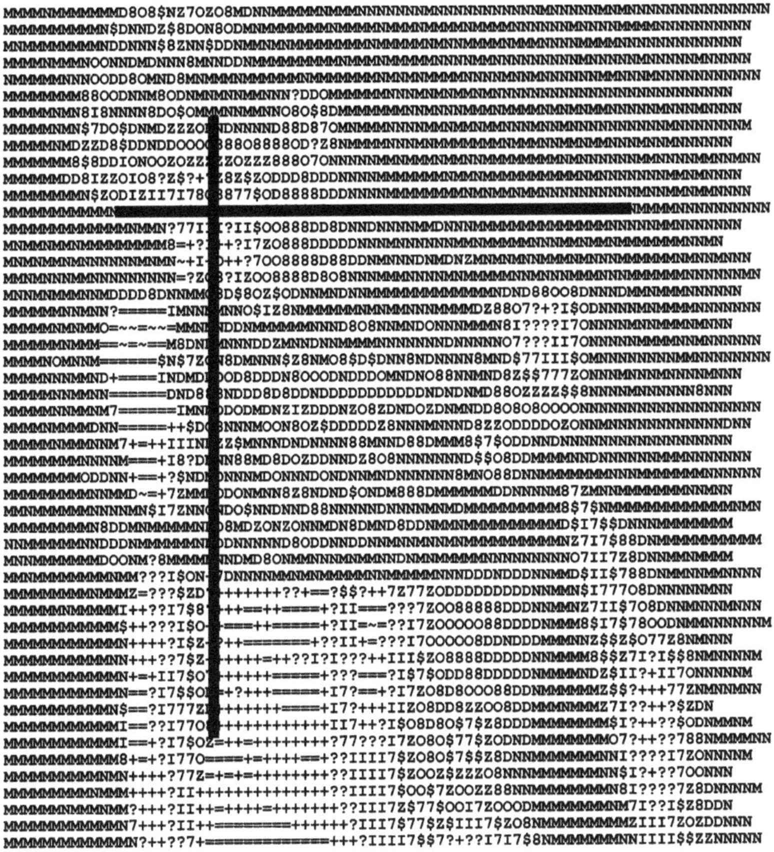

This book was composed by
Chagrin using Zapf Elliptical
and Montserrat fonts.

© Metaflux Publishing 2015

www.metafluxpublishing.com

ISBN 978 0 9933272 2 3

www.ingramcontent.com/pod-product-compliance
Lightning Source LLC
Chambersburg PA
CBHW062151020426
42334CB00020B/2563